Reading in Bed

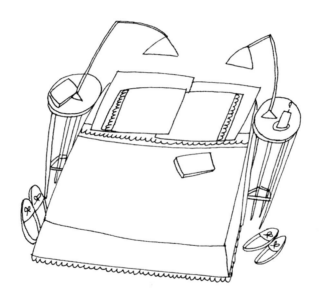

Reading in Bed

Updated Edition

———

Brief headlong essays
about books & writers & reading & readers

———

Brian Doyle

saint mary's press

READING IN BED, Updated Edition
Brief headlong essays about books & writers & reading & readers
by Brian Doyle

Interior drawings by Mary Miller Doyle
Cover design & typesetting by Harvest Graphics
Cover image by Jessy Paston on Unsplash. Used with permission.

Previously published by ACTA Publications, 2015, 2017

9141

ISBN: 978-1-64121-037-9

Printed in the United States of America

*to the avid omnivorous ferocious
reader Joe McAvoy, with thanks
for many years of friendship &
debates about books & writers*

Contents

A Note from the Publisher of This Updated Edition

Was Brian Doyle the most passionate essayist in America? I don't know, but he was the most passionate writer I ever worked with. Also one of the most prolific. And most talented. Brian died in May of 2017 at age sixty after a short but determined fight with brain cancer. He was for many years the editor of *Portland* magazine, the award-winning publication of the University of Portland.

Brian gloried in his many vocations as a husband and father of three, a son and brother, a friend of multitudes, an editor and writer, a coach and mentor to young people. He wrote about daily stuff, mostly: the world of work, family, church, community, and nature. In this book in your hands, he wrote simply about reading and writing, two of my favorite subjects.

I have been publishing books for over thirty years and have worked with literally hundreds of writers. None have been as much fun to work with as Brian. He made me laugh many times, but then he made me cry just as often to balance things off.

Brian wrote so much and so well and so intensely that publishers could not keep up with him. Just among "Catholic" publishers, he wrote for at least the following book publishers: Ave Maria Press, Corby Books, Franciscan Communications, Liturgical Press, Loyola Press, Orbis Books, Paulist Press, and my own ACTA Publications—not to mention the countless religious and secular magazines and other book publishers he wrote for all over the globe. He would explain to all of us that his three kids insisted on eating and that his wife concurred with them.

When Brian first sent me his proposals for two books of essays that became *Grace Notes* and *So Very Much the Best of Us*, I couldn't say yes fast enough. I don't get a lot of literary rock stars coming to my small publishing house. But then began my education in how to work with him as a writer.

It's not so much that Brian had an ego. He certainly did, but it was well-earned. No one could turn a phrase or pull on a heartstring or make you laugh out loud the way he could. But my education came from dealing with him as a writer who had definite opinions about *editing*. I wasn't used to that. Most of my authors are simply delighted to have a publisher (any publisher?), and they seem to want me to edit their books to make them "better." Not Brian. For him it was not enough for me to change something to make his writing "better." I had to prove that it was, in fact, "better" and not just "different."

So my first efforts with him were less than successful. I'd edit an essay and send it to him with the changes "tracked." He'd send it back to me with most of my "suggestions" deleted and restored to his original. Then I'd try to explain to him why I had suggested what I had. Here were some of the reasons he would not accept: His writing did not follow my publishing house's style sheet. ("Who said a publisher had to have a style sheet?") Some of his sentences were rather long and convoluted. ("So what? Readers are smart and will figure them out!") He made up words that aren't even in the dictionary. ("How do you think dictionaries get their new words?")

Eventually I found a way to work with Brian that we both could live with: I accepted 95% of what he wrote initially. (I realized that he really was a gifted writer and that the people who liked his writing also liked his experiments with language. You will too.) Where I really thought a change was needed, I would show Brian the change and explain why I wanted to make it. (The main arguments that seemed to work with him were either that it made what he was trying to say clearer to the reader or that it was funnier than what he had written.) And when I couldn't convince Brian that a change was needed, I deferred to his judgment. (This made the entire editing process go a lot easier and quicker. And besides, he was usually right.)

It was after I started editing him this way that Brian once announced (not publicly) that I was a "good editor." In this updated edition of *Reading in Bed*, originally published by Corby Books, I didn't have to do much editing. It had already been done, in large part by Jeff Baker, then the book editor for *The Oregonian* where many of these essays were first published, whose original Introduction to this book I have left intact, although it carries a special poignancy now. Even so, I did find a few typos (at least I think they were typos, although maybe Brian was creating new words or grammar, as he was wont to do) and corrected them, putting me forever in Brian's category of "meticulomaniacs."

I miss Brian. The world does too. But he did leave a body of great writing for all of us to enjoy, including the list on the final page of this book containing 30 titles by him that are presently in print. Brian would be pleased if we all read every one of them, preferably but not necessarily in bed.

Gregory F. Augustine Pierce
Publisher, ACTA Publications

Introduction
by Jeff Baker

When Brian asked me to write an introduction to what he called his "bookishness collection of bookish essays almost all of which you published, you poor nut," I knew it was the perfect time to exact revenge for all those times I had to defend his run-on (and on) sentences against the copy desk.

Sure, I told Brian, no problem. And by the way, I'm on a bit of a Hemingway kick. I just finished Paul Hendrickson's wonderful *Hemingway's Boat*, and it took me back to *Green Hills of Africa* and *Men Without Women*. I'll write the intro in Hemingway's early style, as a contrast to yours. How's that sound?

I didn't have to wait long for a response: "Hahahaha that poor man, deluged by periods. Periods are fascist."

There you have it: in three words, surely the shortest sentence he's ever written, is Brian's artistic credo, and a better title for this book than whatever 93-word monstrosity he came up with. *Periods are fascist*. It should be on a plaque on his desk. It'll surely be on his tombstone. Say it, and you owe him a nickel.

Periods are fascist.

There, another five cents to Brian. But don't worry. He's not in this for the money. He once told me that too, right after he asked why his payment was late. (It wasn't.) If you read the correspondence of any writer — the complete letters, not the selected — you'll find that 87.4 percent of it is about money, asking for it, worrying about it, complaining about it, asking for it again...

But I digress, and I just wrote a sentence that's a poor imitation of one of Brian's. Once his essays caught on in *The Oregonian*, I began getting queries from freelancers suggesting a short essay on this or that offbeat topic. Nobody mentioned him by name, but the implication was clear: if Doyle can do it, so can I. (They couldn't.) It's not easy writing a sentence that starts in Ireland and ends in Australia, two of Brian's favorite places, and has three semicolons, a parenthetical digression about Van Morrison or Ursula K. Le Guin or Dwayne Wade (or all three, compared and contrasted) and an ellipsis at the end.

But never a period: *periods are fascist.* (Cha-ching!)

Brian started writing for *The Oregonian* years ago as a regular reviewer, reviewing regular books. One day he sent in an (unsolicited) essay about apostrophism or reading in bed or reading refrigerators or something. I fought off the copy editors who really, really liked it but just wanted to make this one long sentence into seventeen short ones, and we published it pretty much as written. People liked it. Brian liked the response he received. We did it again, and again. He asked if he could send one whenever the mood struck him, and I could run it whenever the mood struck me. The word "transom" was used, as in "send it over the transom." (How charmingly old school is that expression? Does anyone even have a transom anymore?)

The next thing I knew, I had five bookish essays in the queue, and plenty more where those came from. Brian occasionally asks how many I'm holding (the answer is always four), then sends another one. People love them. The copy desk loves them. *You'll* love them, once you accept that the respected editor of an award-winning magazine and the author of all sorts of weirdly delightful books really does believe that periods are fascist.

In the old days, back when doors had transoms and editors wore green eyeshades, reporters ended their stories with this notation:

– 30 –

It means that's it, end of story, stop right there. It says a lot about Brian and his work that he would blow right through it, laughing all the way.

———

Jeff Baker is a freelance writer and editor in Portland, Oregon.

I.
NOTES ON
READING

Books in Cars

While rummaging in my car the other day I discovered Eudora Welty and James Herriot pressed together intimately in the trunk, which I bet is a sentence never written before, and while of course my first thought after finding them face to face was who would win a fistfight between Eudora Welty and James Herriot's wife Joan, the Mississippian being one of those sinewy wiry country types and the Englishwoman being a strapping beefeater, my *next* thought was I wonder if anyone other than me carries books in their cars in case of reading emergencies and unforeseen opportunities, so I took it upon myself to ask, being a responsible literary citizen, and the answer turns out to be pretty much yes, which is really interesting, as is the vast list of books themselves, which included dictionaries, novels, atlases, cookbooks, phone directories, comic books, histories, biographies, audio-books, manuals of all sorts, bibles, wine-tasting notes, books of knitting patterns, books of sheet music, books about breastfeeding, and a handbook on vipassana meditative practice.

A naturalist in Hawaii had two notebooks of her own research into how one in five albatrosses is gay and only female frigate birds are thieves. A man in Vermont had a scuba diving manual. A novelist had Evelyn Waugh and *The Rules of Golf*. A chancellor had comic books. Zane Kesey had a copy of his dad's glorious novel *Sometimes a Great Notion*. A dentist had books about railroads and circuses. A publisher had twenty copies of one of the books he had published. A doctor had only books by doctors. A great novelist had forty pounds of string quartet music. A bookseller had exclusively books by Sherman Alexie. A woman in Alaska had every single book she owned because she was moving from one apartment to another. A winery owner had wine-tasting notes which he noticed were all garbled at the end. A poet had a book about Athanasius Kircher and photocopies of every poem written by William Stafford between the years 1937 and 1948. A baseball maniac had David Shield's oddly hilarious *Baseball Is Just Baseball*, the gnomic sayings of Mariners' outfielder Ichiro Suzuki. A friend in Australia had *The Story of the Melbourne Cricket Ground*, which she discovered belonged to an early husband. A fine novelist had James Welch, Flannery O'Connor, and copies of two of his own books to give away on the spur of the moment. The greatest travel writer in the world, Jan Morris, had dictionaries in French, Spanish, German, and Italian. The great novelist Tony Hillerman had Hemingway's *A Farewell to Arms*. One woman in London had books about Margaret Thatcher and rats, a fascinating juxtaposition, and another had *Baby's First Catholic Bible* and *Salmon Fishing on the Yemen*, another interesting juxtaposition. One priest carried a manual on how to preside over last rites and another priest had books about how to preside over weddings and how to grow camellias. A friend in Canada had books about tractors and sake. Another friend in Canada had Nietzsche's *Ecce Homo*. Another friend had a book by H.P. Lovecraft and a book about learning Latin. A friend in Belize had a novel in Belizean English, as he said, which began with a man being tied to a pole on the beach. A great poet had *Junior the Spoiled Cat* and *Teddy Bear of Bumpkin Hollow* in her car, maybe for her grandchildren but maybe not. A young father of triplets had three copies of *Pat the Bunny* by Dorothy Kunhardt, which has sold six million copies since it was first published in 1940. A historian in Texas had a book on the history of zero and another book about the square root of negative 1, which makes you wonder about historians and Texas. A friend in California had books on alcoholism and Lutheranism. A friend in Oregon has *Backpacking with Mule or Burro*, which he liked especially, he said, because it had a chapter on how to persuade your wife to backpack with a mule or burro. A friend in Ohio had Doctor Seuss and a book about dismembering deer. A woman in Louisiana had Batman comics and *Hiking with Jesus*. Another woman in Louisiana had a copy of *The Encyclopedia of U.S. Army Patches, Flashes, and Ovals* — "don't even ask," she said, so I didn't.

Pretty much every other person I talked to had overdue library books (one man had more than sixty) in the car, and pretty much everyone with overdue library books thanked me for making them remember their overdue library books, which they were absolutely going to return posthaste, but I bet they didn't. Eleven people had Bibles of various translations, one man had a Gideon Bible he claimed to have borrowed from a motel, one woman had a Tao Te Ching, and one man, not a priest, carried an Italian-language Catholic missal; interestingly not one person had a Book of Mormon, which Mark Twain, bless his testy heart, memorably called pretentious, sleepy, insipid, tedious, a mess, a mongrel, and chloroform in print, among other compliments. But then no one had a Qur'an either, or a psalm book, or a memoir of seven-fingered circus performers in Samoa, so there you go.

Among the authors represented in cars are the greats (Borges, Chekhov, Agatha Christie, Beverly Cleary, Don DeLillo, Scott Fitzgerald, Hemingway, Maugham, Thurber, Yeats), the very goods (Richard Flanagan, Joseph Mitchell, Philip Roth, J.K. Rowling, George Saunders, Colm Toibin, and the late Kurt Vonnegut), the goods (Eggers, Kerouac, Kingsolver, Lamott, Quindlen), and many whom I am not qualified to qualify, like Margaret Mitchell and Brian Jacques and Julia Child and Georges Simenon, you could get into endless roaring pub arguments here, asking dangerous questions like, Is *Gone With the Wind* the most popular bad book ever written? and If millions of people flip through Julia Child every day does that make her a great writer? and Are Brian Jacques and writers like him who wake up millions of kids to stories really the most influential and cool writers ever far more than people like James Joyce? and Is Georges Simenon a great writer for having created a vast saga of French life and character or was he, like G.K. Chesterton and Thomas Merton, one of those poor scribblers who never had an unpublished thought? But I am not going to ask those questions publicly, not me.

In the end the single best-represented author in cars was Theodor Seuss Geisel, whose books far outnumbered those of any other author in the cars of the people I spoke to, although to be honest most of the people I spoke to were parents who either had kids young enough to relish the good Doctor, or they, the parents, had never actually cleaned the Doctor Seuss books out of the car after their kids went off to college or to join the circus in Samoa or whatever. It cheers me up to think of all those Doctor Seuss books in all those cars; somehow the world doesn't seem quite so bruised and brooding once you know that in a reading emergency you can reach under your seat and pull out David Donald Doo or the Katzes from Blooie to Prooie, not to mention Sally Spingel Spungel Sporn. And right there, with the wild music of one of the greatest of American writers of all ringing in our ears, let us drive on into the rest of the day.

On Reading in Bed

Which we have all done, idly or assiduously, thoroughly or haphazardly, in sickness and in health, for richer or poorer, and may well do until death do us part from the teetering pile of novels we have been reading in bed since last summer, drooling on the pages as we fall asleep, propped on one arm, our spectacles surfing down our noses, until the moment that we snap awake suddenly and for a split second wonder where exactly we are, and why we are naked, and who drooled on Dostoyevsky.

But there are many happy hours when we are stark raving awake, and find ourselves reading happily in the broad beam of the bed — in the morning here and there, when no one is around to sound the sluggishness alarm; and in the afternoon sometimes, before a nap, for twenty delicious inky minutes; and occasionally in the evening, if cooking duties have been evaded successfully for religious reasons, and there is a parenthetical hour when you can curl up and knock off a hundred pages off, say, the endless tomes of W.L.S. Churchill, who apparently never had an unpublished thought, the poor badger.

Some books should be read in bed — Proust, for example, who seems to have spent most of his adult life writing in bed, and Robert Louis Stevenson's *A Child's Garden of Verses*, which was composed in bed, and which eerily lends itself to being read there, and which has probably been read aloud by supine parents to their sleepy children more than any book in our language, except the stoner classic *Goodnight Moon*. And some magazines, I notice, are best read in bed, for murky reasons: *The New Yorker*, for example, and *National Geographic*, maybe because they are small enough to handle easily and clean enough not to leave inky evidence in the bed, which is why we don't read the Sunday newspaper in bed anymore, do we, having learned our lesson that time Prince Valiant's face was discovered imprinted on the pillow, boy, was that hard to explain.

Moving on, there are the simple pleasures of reading in bed, to wit being bare of foot and sans of trousers, and there are the logistical conundra, to wit getting the book propped securely amidships and persuading the reading lamp to stop nodding sleepily (band-aids are good, although I know of people who use gum and duct tape), and there is the ancient problem of glancing at the book that your bed companion is reading and getting absorbed in it surreptitiously over her shoulder and wishing she would turn the page faster dang it and then when she gets up to check on the children, quickly snatching it and zooming through a few pages and trying desperately to remember what page she was on before she comes back to bed and gives you that look you know all too well, the look that nearly killed the refrigerator repairman that time, let's not bring that up again.

But these are small problems with which we are all familiar, whereas there are some larger challenges, such as what if you are reading Ian Frazier and you start laughing so hard there's an accident? and what if you are reading Ann Coulter and you lose your temper and your head flies off, would insurance pay for that? and what if you are reading something unbearably dull and you get the irrepressible urge to leap out the window and run down the street naked as Will Ferrell, will anyone visit you in jail?

In conclusion, reading is bed is a grim responsibility, I believe, and as a society we fail our children if we do not carefully remove our street clothes, don cotton pajamas of any hue, and crawl into the boat of the bed with a sigh of delight, each and every night, there to voyage into the glory of story, UnKindled, BlackBerryless, PalmPilot-less, with our spectacles sliding ever so gently down our probiscii, our minds opening gently like steamer clams, hoping against hope that the Companion will brush her teeth for a really long time tonight so we can bump off the rest of her chapter, while trying to remember, with what is left of the soft ice cream of our minds, that she was on page ninety. We hope.

Your Life List: or, What to Read When

Age one: *Pat the Bunny*. Arguably the most intimate reading experience of your lifetime. Read it every night with your parents. Where's the bunny? *There's* the bunny!

Age two: reread *Pat the Bunny*. Try not to eat the pages this time. Write a paper of no fewer than three pages (single-spaced) on either of these themes: (a) the whole peek-a-boo blanket thing — does Homeland Security know? (b) putting your finger through Mommy's wedding ring, is that an insidious form of heterosexual fascism or a devious placement ad by the bridal industry or what?

Age three: read *Goodnight Moon* while listening to the collected work of Courtney Love on your headphones. Will your head explode? Why or why not?

Age four: you want to ease up a little this year, go on cruise control. Ronald Reagan's letters, the speeches of Marcel Marceau, the list of Elizabeth Taylor's husbands, that sort of thing.

Ages five to nine: free read. Read anything you can reach — comic books, photo books, maps, wanted posters at the post office, sports books, seismographs, the Bible in Hebrew, whatever.

Ages ten and eleven: the whole Harry Potter saga, beginning with *The Seven Major Works* and including *The Three Lesser Tomes*. Write an essay exploring this question: why is it that everyone moos happily that Joanne Rowling has sparked millions of people young and old around the world to read, and people have sprinted to bookstores to buy millions of her riveting books, and her books are so thrilling and deft that a series of films has been spawned from them, but no one ever calls Joanne Rowling of Gloucestershire one of the Great Writers of Our Time? Why is that?

Age twelve: *The Lord of the Rings*, beginning with *The Hobbit*. Do not go on to read *The Silmarillion* and the other ten thousand mythopoetic explorations of Tolkien's world or you will end up stark muttering insane and governor of New Jersey.

Age thirteen: *The Catcher in the Rye*. Try not to spend the rest of the year sneering like Holden Caulfield. Write a paper of no fewer than two pages on how Salinger brilliantly creates a mask of sneeringness to cover an ocean of loneliness. Question: did he totally nail adolescence or what? And what's the deal with hiding in your house in New Hampshire for the next fifty years?

Ages fourteen to eighteen: stuff for school. Write one paper of no more than two pages explaining why Huck Finn, for all its virtues, is not the great American novel, and Twain totally punts the end by having Tom Sawyer arrive to save the day, and a second paper with the thesis that the great American novel is (choose one): Scott Fitzgerald's *The Great Gatsby*, Harper Lee's *To Kill a Mockingbird*, Kurt Vonnegut's *Slaughterhouse-Five*, Joseph Heller's *Catch-22*, Ken Kesey's *One Flew Over the Cuckoo's Nest*, Thomas Pynchon's *Gravity's Rainbow*, or Ray Bradbury's *Fahrenheit 451*.

Age nineteen: *On the Road*. Get it over with. Enjoy the exuberance and adventure and zest and these jazzy United States. Try not to notice that no one actually holds a job or pays for their own gas or treats women with the slightest respect in the book. Try not to dwell on its deep underlying sadness.

Age twenty: welcome to the big leagues. Focus this year: America. This year you can choose any two Mark Twains, John Steinbecks, Willa Cathers, Annie Dillards, Saul Bellows, Ernest Hemingways, William Faulkners, and Flannery O'Connors. By the end of the year you must also have read Cynthia Ozick's *The Shawl*, Barry Lopez's *The Rediscovery of North America*, Art Spiegelman's *Maus*, Ian Frazier's

Great Plains, and anything by Ken Kesey published before 1986.

Age twenty-one: focus this year: Canada, our Neighbor to the North. After reading any five books by Robertson Davies, you can read anything by Margaret Atwood, Farley Mowat, Mordechai Richler, Emily Carr, and Joni Mitchell, but you may not read the lyrics of Neil Young, which will send you back to patting the bunny. I dreamed I saw the knights in armor coming, saying something about a queen, there were peasants singing and drummers drumming and the archer split the tree, God help us all.

Age twenty-two: Scotland, that moist mud puddle north of Manchester! Now that you are legally able to imbibe the whiskey of life, do so on January 25, celebrating Robbie Burns, while reading Robbie Burns aloud until the wee hours, in the company of lots of your friends. Do not eat haggis. Haggis is disgusting. Spend the rest of the year reading the greatest writer who ever wrote English, Robert Louis Stevenson: *Treasure Island, Kidnapped, Jeykll and Hyde, Weir of Hermiston, Child's Garden of Verses, The Merry Men, The Beach at Falesa, Travels with a Donkey,* his letters, and every essay of his you can find. Then sigh with pleasure that he wrote in our language, and pray for his soul, dead too young.

Ages twenty-three to one hundred: read the rest of the world. Start with Giovanni de Lampedusa's *The Leopard*. Write a paper of no more than one page explaining why this is the finest novel ever written, period, except maybe for *The Horse's Mouth*, by Joyce Cary. Thesis: Cary and Lampedusa were the same man, invented by Graham Greene in a fever dream on Capri. Discuss.

Reading the Refrigerator

And yet *another* subtle literature that everyone reads and relishes and savors and snickers at are the enormous vertical pages in our kitchens, the ones nearly as tall as we are, the ones festooned with cartoons and witticisms and comic strips and photographs and essays and articles and letters and early homework misadventures of young residents of the home in which the refrigerator hums, the refrigerator being the fireplace of the 21st century, the warm glow around which everyone gathers until someone, usually the dad, barks *close that door!*

But we do *read* them, don't we, and we pin and post messages on them, and over the years the lesser stories fall off or are removed, sometimes by mortified children and sometimes by a hungry dog, and the better stories adhere — the haunted photograph from September 11, the nephew's wedding day, the first school photographs in which the child has made a concerted effort to stick his tongue in his nose and apparently succeeded, the hilarious clip from Dave Barry, the shivering poem from W.S. Merwin, the berry pie recipe from gramma in her handwriting that looks like it came straight from the seventeenth century, the article about the neighbor's cat who somehow climbed into the massive electric transformer down the street and was either atomized or sent hurtling into the future, the prayer card from the funeral of the terrific priest who baptized the kids, the certificate of mastery on the accordion, the college graduation photo of the woman of the house in which she looks like she is sixteen years old and is clear proof of her Dorian Gray thing, for now, thirty years later, she looks like she is twenty; and etc.

And we read other people's refrigerators, don't we, pausing by them on the way to the water-closet at social engagements, and getting totally absorbed in that photo of a kid who looks weirdly like Benito Mussolini, and the essay by Elwyn Brooks White, who was maybe the greatest essayist America ever hatched, which is a remarkable thing to say, and the bachelor party photograph where one man appears to be wearing a bathtub and another man appears to be trying to grope the waitress, and the flurry of glorious cartoons by Gary Larson, and a little yellowing shrine to Calvin and Hobbes, and not one but two quotes from Mark Twain, and a photograph of a Tibetan kid with a gleaming shaved head and ancient librarian spectacles who you can't place for a moment and then you realize it's His Holiness the Dalai Lama before the poor guy had to flee his country which was promptly eaten by its ancient ravenous neighbor, and there's a column by a local newspaper columnist about his father-in-law which still makes people cry years after it was published, and there's a snippet of a Winston Churchill speech, and the ubiquitous photograph, at least in Portland and environs, of a former mayor showing his plumbing parts to a naked statue which you have to admit doesn't look real surprised, the things that statue has seen...

Think about it a moment — if there's a place in every house that's devoted to stories of every shape and sort and size, that has oceans of prose and photographs, gobs of poetry and paintings, posters and prints, essays and articles, quotes and notes, yards of cards, voices from all over the universe, stories from every corner of the compass, and those stories are read and pondered by all ages and stages of readers every day, well, isn't a refrigerator a kind of large humming book, then? With all sorts of treasures inside? And how many books have such extraordinary added value as being excellent caves for ale and ice cream? And how many books can ever be said to have also housed shoes, spectacles, snowballs, and a former sparrow, as a certain refrigerator of my personal acquaintance has?

The Beauty of the Book

By which I do not mean books that are consciously made to be Beautiful, like coffeetable books the size of dolphins, and books designed to fold open in funky avant-garde ways that make you want to hit the designer in the head with a tennis ball, but the sheer sturdy simple normal workaday loveliness of the run-of-the-mill book, which is of course not run-of-the-mill at all, what with its stitched signatures of salty grainy paper, and the satisfying shouldery heft of its covers, and its crisp engraved illustrations, and wafting redolent ink, and frontispiece and afterword, and indicia and Library of Congress Number, and the often hilariously self-absorbed biographical note about the author (posing shirtless with his two cats outside the writing shed he built himself in Montana), and the thicket of fulsome blurbs on the jacket, or even several *pages* of blurbs in the front, as if the reader *needs* to hear how great the book is from everyone except the bitter Michiko Kakutani of *The New York Times* before beginning to read, doesn't a marching band of blurbs seem sort of insecure, like the publishers are reassuring themselves nervously that they'll make enough profit to build writing sheds in Montana?

And the Note on the Type (Bembo! Garamond! Caslon!), and the epigraph (seemingly always from Johnny Rotten or Gandhi, or both), and the dedication (*to my fourth wife, with thanks for the best seven weeks ever*), and the acknowledgements ("first appeared in Southwest Jackalope State Review, in slightly different form"), and the publisher's logo, which looks like a deer on steroids, and the front-jacket-flap summary of the plot, usually written by a publicist who didn't actually get around to reading the book, or an editor after a Phish concert.

So many subtle and delightful bibliopleasures: the price of the book, for example, which, on hardcover books with bright shiny jackets, is always quietly hidden in spidery type at the tip of the front-jacket-flap, as if the publisher is sort of embarrassed to charge $29.95, and what's with the 95 cents anyway, do they think a lot of people are going to make a decision to buy because it's *not* thirty dollars? Or the credits for author photographs, I read those with high glee, to see who used to be the author's girlfriend. Or the International Standard Book Number, which it turns out was invented by the International Organization for Standardization (*there's* a shadow company for the CIA if ever there was one), and haven't you also had the urge, as I have, while standing in the shadowy far corner of a quiet bookstore on a wet afternoon, to take out your extra-fine pen, and quietly edit the last digit of a book's International Standard Book Number, so that a customer — Michiko Kakutani, say — who buys a copy of Charles Baudelaire is officially recorded in digital history as having purchased *The Wit & Wisdom of Charles Barkley*? Wouldn't that be cool?

And this is not even to delve into the elegant beauties of older tomes, with their imprinted covers and gold leaf, the entwined initials of the author stamped into the cover, the deckle-edged pages and uncut pages of ancient books, the faintest of tissue sheets over the first daguerreotype, the dingbats and doohickeys, the maniacal enormous initial caps to open chapters, the tiny line sketches at the heads of chapters, the loose thread of the binding waving alluringly at the bottom of the spine, what child has not had the overpowering urge to yank that thread, on the off chance that the book would fall apart so fast that there would be piles of words on the floor?

In short, of the savoring of books there is no end, to paraphrase the famous Israeli poet Ecclesiastes, and while we rightly spend most of our time bookwise absorbed by the content therein, we should occasionally pause and salute the package in which prose has been poured. The book is, after all, among the most successful and enduring technologies ever hatched by the mind of man — a sentence that may or may not ever be written about your cool plastic thing with a thousand electric books inside it.

On the Habit of Reading

The thing is, I'd love to move up the ladder to Jorge Luis Borges, to Søren Kierkegaard, to Jose Saramago, but I am constantly distracted by the quirky — the Evelyn Waughs, the Flannery O'Connors, the Ian Fraziers. I set out to read Edward Gibbon and end up reading Edward Abbey. I set out to read Jane Austen and end up reading Paul Auster. I set out to read Thomas Hardy and end up reading the Hardy Boys.

I don't know how this happens.

I make my plans and procure my books and lay them in careful piles by my reading chair, and then I find myself supine on the floor reading an Ian Fleming novel (*Goldfinger*, most recently; one of the best) or the collected works of Saki or the spare prose of Mary Frances Kennedy Fisher, or all the books by Jim Kjelgaard that feature dogs, which it turns out there are a heck of a lot of those, and what books of his that are not about dogs are about otters and beavers and such, it makes you wonder. Or when I set sail toward a breezy read, purposely aiming for operetta rather than *Sturm und Drang*, I suddenly find myself by accident touring the Highlands of Scotland with Samuel Johnson, L.L.D., of London, and his account of the journey leads to me his companion's utterly different account of the *same* journey, Boswell's *Journal of a Tour to the Hebrides*, and that leads me back to a fine John McPhee book about the Hebrides, *The Crofter and the Laird*, and McPhee's ineffable eye for the natural world leads me to Edward Hoagland, whose eye is even sharper, and the crusty Hoagland's essays on the woods of New England lead me to the cheerful Robert Michael Pyle's essays on the woods of the Pacific Northwest, and in reaction to all that water I turn to the desert, where the Desert

Fathers lead me to Thomas Aquinas who leads me to Thomas Merton whose Anglophilia leads me to books about London, among which I discover James Boswell's diaries of his London journeys, and so come full circle, moaning gently.

I don't know how this happens.

Also I get sidetracked by other people's books, which are sort of like other people's meals in a restaurant, you know how whatever *she* ordered always looks better than what *you* ordered, and what you really want to do is just quietly switch plates when she's not looking, and blame it on the waiter, but you can't really do that, or do it more than once per restaurant, but you *can* do that with books, although it turns out people *hate* when you purloin their books, but one thing I have learned as the father of three kids is that you *can* do that to kids from sheer heft and paternal authority, or in an emergency by using the old *I paid for that book!* hammer, and so in this way I have read Carl Hiassen and Cornelia Funke and Blue Bailett and Lemony Snicket and of course the glorious herculean labors of J.K. Rowling, who, you know, everyone talks about how many copies of her books have been sold, but you never hear anyone say what a terrific writer she is, which is certainly the case, I mean, those books will be in print for centuries, and I was so impressed by her classics that I reread Tolkien and C.S. Lewis, and discovered Philip Pullman, and...

I don't know how this happens.

Then there are the books you always were *supposed* to have read but never actually did read, or lied about reading for papers and such in college, like Katherine Anne Porter and Edmund Spenser and all, but who *really* ever read *all* of the Fairie Queen except on a bet or having taken too much medicine, although I did recently while horrendously sick with the flu sentence myself to reading Marcel Proust, who was so egregiously boring that I could only recover with a steady diet of Silver Surfer comics and a stack of *New Yorker* magazines bigger than my head, which after I finished 28 consecutive copies of *The New Yorker* I had an irresistible urge to wear black and buy an island off the coast of South Carolina for some reason.

I don't know how this happens.

And then, if you are like me, when you are standing politely near someone else's bookshelf, pretending to be interested in politics or religion or the many fine distinctions among possible kitchen floor tiles, you not only thoroughly peruse their entire collection, wondering why anyone would bind issues of *Popular Mechanics* and if there's anyone else in the universe who still has books by Alexander Woolcott, and you have the awful urge to just quietly pocket that copy of J.M. Coetzee or Richard Farina or Joyce Cary that you have been looking for since the dawn of recorded time, but mostly you don't.

I don't know how this happens.

"My reading has been lamentably desultory and immethodical," says the odd and colorful essayist Charles Lamb, and I know whereof he writes, for I am the king of the immethodical readers, which habit has led to, among other things, Charles Lamb, who led me to Thomas Macaulay, who led me to Thomas Carlyle, whom I discover wrote of Lamb that "a more pitiful, ricketty, gasping, staggering, stammering Tom-fool I do not know...he is a confirmed, shameless drunkard, tipples till he is utterly mad, and is only not thrown out of doors because he is too much despised for taking [the] trouble," which led me for some reason to reading writers who were also legendary tipplers, like Faulkner and Kerouac and the Raymonds Carver and Chandler, and...

I don't know how this happens.

And also I go on reading jags that start in libraries and bookstores, where you can wander around running your fingers over endless colorful spines of books, and here and there tease one away from the walls of its fellows, and balance it in your hand, and gaze happily at the lurid cover, and read the breathless first page, and how very many times it has happened to all of us that pawing curiously at a book in the library or bookstore had led straight to work of savor and salt that has really mattered in your life — in my case the odd brilliant travel writings of Robert Gibbings, and James Salter's books on flying, and Mary Lee Settle's graceful books, and the collected works of Charles Nordhoff and James Norman Hall, none of which I never would have read if I didn't fingerwander, and...

The fact is that people who adhere to reading agendas, or grace monthly book clubs, or diligently set to reading the works of Jane Austen in order, or read only new novels by women, or only histories of imperial wars, or only the million novels by such graphomaniacs as P.G. Wodehouse and Agatha Christie, well, they awe and amaze me, for my reading lurches hilariously like a drunken sailor, and I sometimes look back on recent reading adventures with amazement, and wonder if those writers who spoke back to back to me have ever even been in the same sentence before: the sweaty Edgar Rice Burroughs and the elegant Pico Iyer, the dusty Homer Davenport and the urbane urban A.J. Liebling, the tall-tale-teller Mark Twain and the meticulous engineer Henry Petroski, who wrote a *totally* riveting book about pencils, you wouldn't think you could write a great book about pencils but you would be wrong, and his pencils reminds me of a book about railroad maps I just read, which was *genius*, and the word *genius* reminds me inevitably of Robert Louis Stevenson, whose *Kidnapped* I just reread, and I swear it was even better than it was when I read it at age twelve, and that Scottishness of that novel set me to reading old Walter Scott, and...

Smelliterature

News item floating under the old proboscis this morning: the American Chemical Society announces a new "sniff test" whereby the slow death of old books can be accurately measured by analysis of aroma; it turns out that the musty murky bookish smell we all know is composed of hundreds of organic compounds being released, in fairly strict chronological order, by the pages and binding. "A combination of grassy notes with a tang of acids and a hint of vanilla over an underlying mustiness," says the Society's report, sounding entertainingly like a wine doofus, before noting that papers containing pine tar and wood fiber are the first to give up the ghost (or gas).

And away sprints my mind, pondering favorite books and their smells, and the adventures evoked by their smells, and the way some books smell like their stories — *Tom Sawyer* smells like summer, doesn't it? And Ray Bradbury's *Dandelion Wine*, the greatest of all American novels about summer, doesn't that smell like fresh-mown grass and someone frying catfish three houses down? And *War and Peace*, doesn't that smell like a vast forbidding winter, bracing and bitter? And Joyce Cary's masterpiece *The Horse's Mouth*, doesn't that smell like London must have smelled between the world wars, fish heads and apple peels and coal smoke and sour ale and a dying empire?

I peel Tim Winton's glorious *Cloudstreet* off the shelf and crack it open and out comes the most redolent sea breeze from the shore of Western Australia; I open the poems of William Stanley Merwin of the Island of Maui, and out wriggle the sensual allures of mango and guava and koa; I pick up the wonderful essayist Elwyn Brooks

White, and faintly I smell the kelp and workboats and henhouses of his rock-ribbed farm on the coast of Maine...

It's startling, really, the sensory load that books carry. Not all of them, certainly, especially now, when so many new books smell only of money or the itch for it, or of political rage, which smells like frustration, or fear, or a desperate thirst for attention — but many, maybe even most; and this is not only the province of fiction. Edward Hoagland's journals of wandering the moist jungles of northern British Columbia reek of spruce and smoke, Twain's *Life on the Mississippi* of mud and cigars, Mary Oliver's poems of seawrack and scrub pine, Eudora Welty's of shimmering heat and the faint metallic scent of bourbon. Travel writing at its best, of course, is crammed with scent; to read Jan Morris on Hong Kong is to hold a book alive with smell and sound and music and wrangle and burble and the endless howling of car horns, and to read Redmond O'Hanlon's *Trawler* is to smell every kind of awful icy wet weather and dismembered enormous North Sea fish, not to mention the fried candy bars the crew gobbles at every opportunity.

Odd, isn't it, that mere ink on the page, alphabetical parades and processions, stacked in lines and bound with glue, could elicit such a sensory response in the reader, far more than merely the scent-trails of paper and glue changing into gasses, ever so slowly; but that is perhaps the deepest pleasure of all, book-wise, that by diving into the story we change planes, worlds, bodies, time zones, centuries, and without warning we are plunged wholly in another world — plunged so thoroughly that sometimes, wonderfully, thrillingly, we emerge, unsure for a moment where exactly we are. Every reader has had that experience as a child, and loved it, and misses it; but another of the many glories of books is that you can have that extraordinary experience again, today, simply by opening the right book. And there are, as we know with immense joy, so very many of *those*...

A Note on Surreptitiously Reading Other People's Bookshelves

Which you might as well admit right now you have done at least fifty times, and you know exactly what I mean, at parties of every shape and stripe *you*, yes you, have tiptoed gently out of the social ramble and eased infinitesimally into the den or library or living room and happily spent the rest of the party checking out the books, until your paramour tracked you down and sighed, and you drove home silently, your paramour thinking, not for the first time, what an utter doofus you are, and you thinking that you might well have quietly borrowed that lovely old hardback copy of Steinbeck's *Sweet Thursday* without anyone the wiser.

If we are really being honest this morning we would admit that not only do we abrogate our social responsibility when we read other people's bookshelves, the glue of society being chatter and natter, but that we actually do make totally unfair moral judgments about character and taste based on book collections, which we should not do, however tempting it is to think of someone with all of Dan Brown or Jerzy Kosinski as a roaring criminal, and someone with all of Mark Twain or Annie Dillard as a dear friend you do not yet know, despite the fact that Twain committed the sin of *Tom Sawyer Abroad*, and Annie Dillard, bless her large heart, published *The Writing Life*, which even she calls embarrassing.

When I was courting the woman who would later be my wife, she had four books on the bookshelf above her bed, in a tiny apartment near an ocean, and reading her shelves, brief an experience as it was, was a revelatory pleasure: *The Horse's Mouth* by Joyce Cary, *The River Why* by David James Duncan, *The Captain's Verses* by Pablo Neruda, and *The Song of the Lark* by Willa Cather — in other words, three terrific books out of four, the Cather being awful. But still, it seemed to me, it was a very impressive batting average; and then my fate was sealed when I asked, not at all innocently, what her favorite book was, and she said *To Kill a Mockingbird*, and now we have three children.

Anyway, after many years of reading people's shelves I recognize the signs of it in other people, and it is a dark and devious pleasure to be at a party and notice two or three innocents sliding toward the shelves, and to recognize the way people cock their heads sideways when they are scanning shelves, and to snort with laughter at the way a guy will be nodding in agreement at someone's vehement assertion that Scott Spencer's *Endless Love* is the worst book ever written in the history of the world, and suddenly he, the nodding guy, reaches down and pulls out a Walter Mosley novel and says something like *hey! Walter Mosley!* which earns him a glare from his paramour or the host or both, and he has to spend the rest of the party talking about Greg Oden's unfortunate mohawk haircut while I have the stacks blissfully to myself.

Yet there is much to be learned from scanning strange shelves. The alphabetized collection — is that a sign of an orderly mind or of squirming mania? Books arranged by color and/or by height, what does that *mean*? No books at all *anywhere* in a house, what does that *mean*? Books packed so tightly on their shelves that you cannot pry one away from its fellows at all one bit, does that mean no one ever pulls a book out? And what does it mean when you pull out, say, a V.S. Naipaul novel from someone's stacks, and find *LAKE OSWEGO LIBRARY* stamped on the pages? Or when you find a book that *you* loaned the host and you discover he crossed your name out and wrote his own on the flyleaf? Should you just quietly slip it back onto the shelf and amble back toward the onion dip, or should you call Home-land Security?

I remember one house where all the books were novels by women written in the last twenty years, which nags me still, what did that say of the host? And another host who had every single book ever written by P.G. Wodehouse, which is a scary number. And another house which had a remarkable and lovely and comprehensive collection of books, all shelved willy-nilly, Edward Gibbon next to Edward Jones, Ellen Glasgow next to Ellen Gilchrist, Ian McEwan next to Ian Frazier, but over all the shelves a thick dust — not one of those books had been rescued for years. I left that house saddened, and sneezing.

I have even, I confess, wandered strange houses and poked into their bedrooms and clapped eyes on what books were by the beds, even venturing a guess as to who slept on which side by which books were stacked where, and I have spent time in strange bathrooms riffling through the books and magazines people keep there, and in every hotel and motel room I have ever been imprisoned in I have happily pored over the Gideon Bible or the Book of Mormon ("chloroform in print," as Twain called it), and I am so addled by bibliocuriosity that I have spent hours reading the shelves in the offices of doctors of the body, the mind, and the soul, even once choosing a doctor because he had a Robert Louis Stevenson book on his shelves, although it was *Catriona*, the mediocre sequel to Stevenson's masterpiece *Kidnapped*.

In short we all scan other people's shelves, and make unreasonable judgments, and we should cease doing so, because the very fact that people *have* books in their houses is a good thing, all things considered, and we should salute and celebrate that urge, and not care so much what books are there or not there, and if you would do your best to stop reading other people's shelves, I personally would be grateful, because that leaves a little more room for me to poke around. More onion dip?

Summer Reading: a Note

I'll bet you a cheap paperback edition of Robert Louis Stevenson's classic novel *Treasure Island* that (a) you've never actually read it, or (b) you haven't read it since you were twelve years old.

The same goes for Stevenson's terrific novel *Kidnapped*, and Kenneth Grahame's *The Wind in the Willows*, and Madeleine L'Engle's *A Wrinkle in Time*, and Mark Twain's *The Adventures of Tom Sawyer* — all books you read one summer long ago, right? Or maybe you were going to read them but never actually technically did — you had a copy in the house but there was always a game to play or a chore to do, and, well, now you've seen the movie, or your children read it last summer, or you bought lovely edition recently for your grandchildren but didn't shortstop the gift before handing it over...

Here's an idea — read them this summer. They're better than you remember, if you read them before — and if you never read them at all, you'll find them delicious, deft, and delightful. And summer is a perfect time to read them. Instead of gagging on bad loud greedy television, bad loud movies with lots of explosions and unsubtle ads for toys, and bad books by fourth-rate movie stars and fifth-rate spymasters, why not hit the beach with a good book?

The same principle applies to books you might have missed at the ages you should have read them: Jack London's *Call of the Wild* (which should be required reading at age 12), J.D. Salinger's *The Catcher in the Rye* (age 15), Jack Kerouac's *On the Road* (age 19), John Steinbeck's *Cannery Row* and *Sweet Thursday* (which should be read back-to-back at 21 or 22, when readers are old enough to sense that love and pain and laughter are all cousins).

And the same is true of books you were supposed to read in high school or college but never actually *did* quite manage to read, or read hurriedly at best — or only skimmed, or read every third chapter, or just the beginning and end, or asked your roommate for a quick summary, or read the Cliff Notes — any of the million dodges of undergraduates under pressure. "I'll read it later, when I have the time to really read it," you promised yourself.

Now's the time. It's summer — vacations, longer days, looser schedules.

Read Herman Meville's epic *Moby-Dick*, and savor the detail in it, the oceanic sweep of its ambition, the sly humor, Melville's genius for portraying character under pressure.

Or Mark Twain's best book, *Life on the Mississippi*, a funny, artless, open-hearted memoir of his young days as a riverboat pilot. You'll find America in the heady days of its youth, recounted by its finest writer, with sharp-eyed humor and the cheerful affection of an older man for the young man he was.

Or Leo Tolstoy's *Anna Karenina* — you never actually read it, did you? It was the end of the semester, and you had all those papers due, and it was so *thick*, and, well, she couldn't be 600 pages' worth of interesting, right? Wrong — she's as fascinating as any and all women, and you will learn a great deal about women's hearts, and enjoy and suffer along the way, carried easily along by a master storyteller.

Or James Boswell's *Life of Samuel Johnson* — the best biography ever written. Or Virginia Woolf's *Mrs. Dalloway*, another exquisite sort-of-biography.

Or, by golly, James Joyce's *Ulysses* — probably the all-time undisputed champion of books that are supposed to be great but no one actually reads. (Although Tolstoy's *War and Peace* is up there.) News flash: *Ulysses* is great. It's funny, sad, moving, piercing, one of the truest novels ever written, and you'll recognize half the characters in it as people you see and hear every day, even though they are wandering around Dublin on a June day in 1904.

Or Steinbeck's *Grapes of Wrath*, Gustave Flaubert's *Madame Bovary*, Stevenson's *Dr. Jeykll and Mr. Hyde* (far superior to its current incarnation as a musical, and a book that came to its author whole in a dream), E.B. White's *One Man's Meat*, George Orwell's *Animal Farm* (chilling), Joseph Conrad's *Heart of Darkness* (more chilling), Dalton Trumbo's *Johnny Got His Gun*, Erich Remarque's *All Quiet on the Western Front* (most chilling).

Even locally, in the literature of the Pacific Northwest, there are many books that we were *going* to read but never actually opened — books that richly reward reading now, some of them classics that will be in print for centuries. Ursula Le Guin's novel *Left Hand of Darkness*, for example, or her eerie novel set in a future Portland, *The Lathe of Heaven*. Barry Lopez's inimitable *Arctic Dreams*, which won the National Book Award. Tom Robbins' hilarious early novel *Another Roadside Attraction*. Stewart Holbrook's entertaining and informative *Holy Old Mackinaw*, "a natural history of the American lumberjack." Ken Kesey's novels *One Flew over the Cuckoo's Nest* (everyone's seen the excellent movie, but the book's better) and *Sometimes a Great Notion* — the best novel ever written about Oregon, period. Norman Maclean's *A River Runs Through It* — as beautiful and moving a short book as you will ever read, I promise, and again a ton better than the movie, which wasn't half bad.

I cannot resist also advising cheerfully that we continue to avoid some books that we are supposed to have read — the novels of James Fenimore Cooper, for example, which are jaw-droppingly awful, or those of Nathaniel Hawthorne, or of Henry James, whose novels are brilliant and boring. But I hear the screams of many English teachers in the distance, and desist insulting the canon.

But I remain insistent about the startling joy of reading in summer, and I do not mean reading the self-help muck that occupies this week's best-seller list. I mean books that have been selling for dozens or hundreds of years — books you know but never quite consumed, books you read three decades ago, books that are self-help books if what you want to feed is your head and heart. Read 'em this summer. Think of it as a vacation from pop culture, which will lurch along desperately from fad to fad without you while you settle in for a weekend visit with Mister Twain or Ms. Le Guin.

I cannot prescribe all this literary medicine for the doldrums of summer without partaking of it myself — on my reading table this summer is Charlotte Bronte's *Wuthering Heights*, which I never *quite* got to in college, and Willa Cather's *O Pioneers!*, which I thought I detested but never actually read, I discover. (I *hate* that.) And looming like skyscrapers in the distance are six novels by a writer much discussed in recent years but never yet read by the undersigned, despite a lifetime of bookishness — Miss Jane Austen.

Next summer, maybe.

A Note on Finally Being Ready for Some Books, Thank Heavens

And *another* thing all readers know about reading but we hardly ever mention about reading is how sometimes you have to be ready for a book's salt and swing, you have to be prepared lifewise for it to speak to you, and if you read it at the wrong time, too early or too late, the book just seems clogged and dense and self-indulgent and mannered and foolish, and you just don't get it at all, and privately you conclude that all your friends who mooed with delight over it have lost their little tiny tadpole brains, but you can't say that aloud, much, so when they ask anxiously *what did you think?* you have to lie and say you were about to start it when suddenly you found you only understood Basque, or were arrested for impersonating a cockatoo, or something like that. You know what I mean.

The easy categories of books like this are those you should read young, at certain set ages, like *Treasure Island* at age thirteen, and *The Catcher in the Rye* at fourteen, and *The Lord of the Rings* at fifteen, and *One Flew Over the Cuckoo's Nest* at sixteen, and *On the Road* at nineteen, and those books you should read when you are older and have a deeper sense of pain and grace, like *War and Peace* and *The Grapes of Wrath* — both books that are elephantine and ponderous to the young, but poignant and powerful for people who have grappled with violence and lost sleep over joblessness and moneylessness.

But then there are all sorts of books that you flip open here and there over the years and they just don't *grab* you, you read a couple pages in the quiet redolent aisle of the library or bookstore and you don't have the itch to turn to the third page, and you sigh and put it back on the shelf, but here and there over the years you pick it up again, idly, wondering, and then finally, one day, while waiting for your shoes to dry out, you stake out the good chair in the bookstore and flip it open and this time you get so absorbed you discover you are on page thirty by the time the owner's laser glare registers, and you buy the thing, and read another forty pages on the bus some, and then another fifty pages after dinner, and you end up bringing it to work and reading it in the water closet, desperate to find out what happened to the daughter in Malta, or whatever.

This just happened, for me, with Cynthia Ozick's *The Puttermesser Papers*, which I had tasted here and there over the years and never could eat — it seemed too studiously Jewish and New Yorkish and femaleish to me — until recently, when I started and finally grokked the heroine's nutty courage against loneliness, and the wild creativity of the plot, and the way the story is crammed with detail and idea in same hilariously chaotic brilliant way as Saul Bellow's great *Humboldt's Gift*, say; another book in which the dense narrative deliberately reflects the intricate labyrinthine tendrilling of the seething human brain, not to mention the extraordinary jungle of the heart. And there was a subtle joy in diving into the novel, for me — a tiny hard-to-articulate pleasure that the book and I had finally come to an understanding, so to speak, and would be cheerful companions now for a while, and even after the first flush of enjoyment we would always be happy acquaintances, in the same way you still rather like the people who used to live in your college dorm even though you only see their names and faces in passing every few years.

That happened to me with James Joyce's *Ulysses*, too, which I read first like everybody else, looking for the lubricious parts, and then had to read again in college, dutifully slogging along marking subtle symbolic flourishes with a red pen, but then read a third time when I was Bloom's age, 38, and the third time was the charm — I finally understood the sprawling salty genius of it, the shambling quiet courage of the anti-hero, the incredible capture of some hilarious broken brave seething humanity one day in one city, and even understood that some of it was less than fine — as the Irish novelist Roddy Doyle has said, the Nighttown section is muck, where was the man's editor?

The point, I guess, is that for every book we keep picking up and hurriedly put back down again, convinced yet again that we will never begin to like Thomas Hardy or Ayn Rand, there is one that will finally snag your lapel and command your attention. For me the easiest way to find those books is to wander through the town library, trailing my fingers over the bright and sturdy spines, and acquiescing to accident — by chance I pull a Patrick O'Brian an inch clear of his companions, and glance at the first page, and finally, after many dry years, there is a whiff of salt and sea, and away we go...

A Note on Public Literature

Shuffling happily through a moist murmuring winter day recently I began to notice what we might call Public Literature, the stories and poems and essays and bromides and rants and shouts and gnomic tales published on buses and walls and signs and trains and telephone poles, and I have spent weeks now jotting notes on the songs they sing: the terse commands posted along highways and byways, for example, such declarative sentences, such blunt and inarguable instructions, *yield* and *wrong way* and *merge*; and the huge shouted poems rattling by me on the elephantine flanks of light-rail trains; and the epic photographic essays and sales pitches unfurled on billboards, with their grim gimlet-eyed sports teams and pints of ale thirty feet deep and immense work boots suitable for goliaths; and the wildly colorful jitterbug of graffiti (my all-time favorite, *CHE WAS GHE!*), and the bright repetitive chants of political signs, their patronymic insistence a sort of poem or prayer flag...

And then there is the taut literature of bumper stickers and the other ephemera people glue to their cars, sometimes so many stickers and decals and signs and symbols that you find yourself unconsciously tailgating so as to be able to read more thoroughly, or praying for a stoplight so you can try to make out what the driver or owner or thief might be saying thematically with truck-buttocks advertising politicians, opinions, rodeos, colleges, rock bands, radio stations, and the fact that someone in the family used to be on the honor roll in elementary school, although that particular sticker is mostly peeled off, perhaps from honoree embarrassment, or because the former honoree is now thirty years old and running a tiki bar in Bora Bora.

Consider the signs in and on and over stores, the signs in windows, posters, prints, broadsheets, the messages we print and scrawl for each other and pin up on the village green, in the many forms that arena takes; for all we laud and fear the electric village, we still talk to each other volubly in public, and while that conversational river is mostly commercial, there are also extraordinary moments of grace and pain, moments of quiet literature — the glowering most-wanted men in the post office, the plaintive request for help with a missing cat on the grocery billboard, the smiling faces of lost or kidnapped children on milk cartons, the often-hilarious but sometimes haunted tiny novels in the personals section of the newspaper, the terse epic literature of the police log, the entertaining soap opera of the minutes of the city council meeting — which used to be posted on the walls of city hall where I live, and I loved to stop by sometimes and read them, as I wandered home with armfuls of diapers, and try not to fall down laughing in the hallway at the published posturing and machination, because the floor there was really hard, and I hated to disturb the labor of harried clerks by laughing so hard I must have sounded like a man with a weasel in his pancreas.

And the banners trailing behind small sputtering airplanes in summertime, and the smoke stories airplanes write in the air sometimes, the roman type becoming italic with the wind; and the blinking neon lights on which sometimes a letter or two winks out and you are left with a brilliant sudden poem where there had been only information before; or the bedsheet banners and cardboard statements people hang from highway bridges sometimes, the sweetest being birthday greetings, and, once, on a shimmering summer morning, a marriage proposal, to which about every other car that passed under it honked happily *yes! yes!*

And the post-it notes we leave for each other and for our unmemorious selves, so often poignant little poems, like *milk / cheese / cookies / love / mom*; and the finger-painted words and pictograms on steamed bathroom mirrors and car windows; and the words fingered onto truck-walls slathered with a month of dust; and posted memos and rules and regulations and rosters; and the poem of the all-time track records in the history of the school mounted by the gymnasium; and the fluttering poem of the league championship flags riffling by the skylight; and the alphabetic parade marching around four walls of the kindergarten, pausing only to allow the door to open and the fresh minds to wander in...

Posters and prints, letters and lectures, speeches and song lyrics, newspaper clippings and magazine covers, maps and charts and graphs and diagrams, famous and infamous quotes, ticket stubs and funeral notices, and best of all the scrawled glorious heartfelt notes and letters and early headlong essays of children — all these things are public literature, are they not? Each a story, each soaked with meaning and emotion, each something that when you touch it or notice it afresh or are asked to explain it, out pours a tale very often exactly the shape of your heart...

Why Portland, Oregon, Is the Coolest Literary City in the West

I have worshipped the holy air where Erickson's Workingman's Club used to burble and roar, on Burnside Street between Second and Third avenues, because it was in that echoing wooden emporium, in that that legendary saloon with its vast planked floors punctured by many thousands of hobnails, that the second-greatest Portland writer of them all, the glorious Stewart Holbrook, once held court, chaffing and razzing, teasing and grinning, listening and lecturing, until he ceased to imbibe because visions of snakes and bats were granted unto him, though there were technically no snakes and bats in his immediate personal area, so he desisted from the water of life and its many devious ands wondrous cousins, and retired posthaste, but not before mulling and then milling a thousand stories from the dense air of Erickson's, which is why every time I shuffle past where it used to be I stop and make obeisance, for which I once got stared at by a suspicious cop, who told me to scurry along, which I did.

I have shaken the enormous horny hand of the late astounding Ken Kesey on Morrison Street. I have shaken the deft calm hand of the genius Barry Lopez on Davis Street. I have shaken the tiny prolific hand of the polymath Ursula Le Guin on Fifteenth Avenue near where she has lived for many years. I have shaken the hand of tall quiet gentle John Daniel on Princeton Avenue where he lived for many years. I have shaken the brave papery hand of the late Alvin

Josephy on Salmon Street, and that was a hand that once belonged to the United States Marine Corps and clenched a rifle in the heat and blood and rage and fear and courage and chaos and fury of Guadalcanal and Iwo Jima, a fact of which I was very much aware at the time, despite the kind eye and amused seamed face of that most interesting Oregon writer, whose hand was as warm and friendly as he was.

I have walked the streets in northeast Portland where Beverly Cleary was a girl, and you cannot tell me that there was ever a finer writer in the history of Portland than Beverly Cleary, because not only do her many books sing and laugh and ramble and burst with real people and excellent dogs and joy and tears and the dense emotional thickets of childhood, but they have been read by millions of children, which is a remarkable thing to say, and I might argue, if we in a good pub with excellent ale and no hurry, that waking the hearts and brains and litry hungers of children is the very best thing any writer can do, which is another reason why Robert Louis Stevenson is the best writer in the history of the English language, because who among us who were raised in the ocean of that ancient tongue has not been lulled to peaceful slumber, and lulled his or her children to ditto, by the thin grinning Scot's glorious *Child's Garden of Verses*?

I rest my case.

But I am wandering away from my city. I have wandered the shaggy rumpled streets of Saint Johns, with that loveliest of bridges leaping above me as I wondered which lanes and alleys once held the young Gary Snyder in their stony embrace. I have ambled southeast Portland where the lean leathery smiling Robin Cody lives. I have wandered past *The Oregonian* building on Broadway where Ben Hur Lampman hatched his inimitable small lyrical essays and the deadpan storycatcher Steve Duin does so today. I have shuffled past the spot in Washington Park where John Reed grew up. I have rambled along Vista Avenue thinking I was swimming through the air where once the polymath Charles Erskine Scott Wood wandered and pondered.

And I have read and heard and seen and laughed with and been startled by and awakened by and moved by Monica Drake and Karen Karbo and Kim Stafford and Sallie Tisdale and Molly Gloss and Diana Abu-Jaber and Charles D'Ambrosio and Whitney Otto and James Hall and Brian Booth and Gus Van Sant and Walt Curtis and Barbara La Morticella and Joanne Mulcahy and Ana Callan about a hundred more Portland writers I cannot remember at the moment because I am a man inundated by children and thus rimrocked by laundry and riddled by dishes to be done.

Suffice it to say that this city, Stumptown and Timbertown, Puddletown and the City of Roses, the city hatched by a coin flip and blessed by the rain, the city riven by waters and huddled by hills, the city with the greatest independent bookstore in the world, the city where a mayor exposed his woodpecker to a naked statue, the city where you can still to this day catch a salmon bigger than a child in the river that runs through it, the city that wasn't supposed to be a great city because the great city was supposed to be miles upriver but it didn't happen that way, well, suffice it to say that this city is a city stuffed with stories unending and wonderful, salty and moist, hilarious and haunting, and some of the greatest writers this country ever hatched have lived and worked here, spinning their tales and yarns, which makes me inordinately proud; I mean, really, in the end, what have we to exchange that matters, except stories of grace and courage, laughter and love?

A Note on Seriesousness

Just finished a headlong dash through the eleven novels of C.S. Forester's legendary Horatio Hornblower series, and even as the addled mud of my mind swirls with cannon fire and sea mist and the epic clash of British ships against the brooding tyrant Napoleon Bonaparte (that cruel diminutive first draft of Hitler), I pause to contemplate the pleasures of reading *series* of books, the parades of linked stories that ultimately compose vast novels of thousands of pages.

Because, really, are there not many subtle pleasures in serial books? The realization, at the end of Book One, that you have stumbled on a gripping tale, beautifully told, and there are many alluring islands ahead to be visited; the happy workmanlike feeling of being in the middle of the series, and having a firm grasp of the cast of characters, and knowing there are books enough waiting for you that the summer will whir past like a nighthawk; the dichotomous sense of hungrily wanting to *know* what's going to *happen* while mourning quietly that there are only a few pages left in the whole *saga*; the sigh of satisfaction at the very end, not only that you have actually read eleven consecutive novels and savored every moment of the journey, but that you now have, let's say, Captain Hornblower, or Legolas, or Lyra Belacqua, or V.I. Warshawski, or (god help us all) Sir Harry Flashman as a shadowy friend the rest of your life, as yet another example of the mysterious awkward grace of the human animal, because the best fictional characters are utterly *true*, isn't that so?

Braces of books like John Steinbeck's undeservedly uncelebrated masterpieces *Cannery Row* and *Sweet Thursday*; trilogies like Philip Pullman's *His Dark Materials*, quartets like Paul Scott's haunting account of the end of the British Raj in India or J.R.R. Tolkien's masterpiece *The Lord of the Rings* (in which *The Hobbit* is really the opening book, yes?), sprints of seven like C.S. Lewis' Narnia novels or the tale of Mr. H. J. Potter of 4 Privet Drive, sprawling piles like the late George MacDonald Fraser's twelve hilarious Flashman novels, or incredible mountains like the more than fifty Inspector Maigret novels by Georges Simenon — it's a fascinating subgenre of fiction, the series. And while many series are carried along by a single (and singular) character, others have immense circles of casts, layers of voices, hints and intimations of endless more tales to be told; and perhaps this too is a secret of great literature, that the best novels are those that give a reader the sense of seeing and hearing only *part* of the world created within those covers; in a really fine book, say an enormous novel like Fraser's collected Flashmania, you get a powerful sense of the tumultuous thrum of people beyond the margins of the page, characters walking away to live their lives unaccounted by the present author, a thousand stories beneath the one on the page...

Another virtue of the series, it seems to me, is that very often this is where young readers enter the seething and delightful universe of books, in a way that sets them up for life as readers; the many wonderful books you read as a small child are not read with quite the same intent fervor that my teenage daughter, for example, has consumed a book a day when she is on a tear through one of the many series of teenage romance novels she reads — I am never quite sure of their titles and authors, as they come and go so fast that all I see clearly is their shocking pink and roaring yellow covers. All teenage romance novels have covers in lurid nuclear colors, why is that?

Anyway, I sing the pleasures of seriesousness, from modest twins (even if slightly forced into companionship, like Truman Capote's terrific Thanksgiving and Christmas memories) all the way to the inexhaustible ocean of, say, Agatha Mary Clarissa Miller Christie, who sold more books than anyone in history except the anonymous geniuses who wrote the Bible and the retired actor from Stratford in

Warwickshire. To dive into a series, and find yourself absorbed, and flip back to the frontispiece, where you discover there are *eight more novels like this* — that is yet another of the quiet but delicious delights of the world of books, a world that at its very best reveals the deepest bones and sweetest songs of this world, don't you think?

Booklessness

Confession: I have loaned books I didn't like to people knew would never return them in this lifetime, *while making a point of how much I wanted to get the books back*. I have accidentally on purpose left books at people's houses and in pubs and in playgrounds and in the library. I once left a book (one of John Updike's 900 novels about infidelity, did the man never write about anything but neurotic infidelity in autumn?) in a church. I have thrown a book (Jerzy Kosinski's awful *Blind Date*) into a woodchipper. I once tried to feed a copy of the Good News Bible, in which all the glorious shouldery dense muscular prickly thorny edgy epic language of the King James Bible was beaten into happy fluff, to a small cow in Rochester, Minnesota, but the cow did not bite, perhaps for reasons of literary taste, and her owner was alarmed and suspicious, so we left, my friend and me, although we later left the book at a Dairy Queen.

I once left a book by Bill McKibben (*Maybe One: A Case for Smaller Families*) in a meeting room of the Church of Jesus Christ of the Latter-day Saints, just to see what would happen. (I found it neatly shelved the next day in proper alphabetical order, which seems sweet.) I once left Heidegger's *Being and Time* in a kindergarten class, to see what would happen. (I found it a few days later helping to hold up a hamster cage, certainly the best work that old Nazi ever did.) I once left a Silver Surfer comic (one of the series where he is a melancholy wanderer through the cosmos, dreaming of his first love Shalla-Bal) in a university theology department office. I have done these things, and I am not proud of them.

On the other side of the coin, I have scrounged desperately for books when I had no books, for example on trips where you have read too fast and are in the hotel with nothing whatsoever to read except the Gideon Bible. I once was trapped in a motel in Utah with nothing but the Book of Mormon, which was the closest experience I have had in this life to dropping acid, and which sent me, as soon as I made it home, to digging up Twain's entertaining notes on the book: "...chloroform in print. If Joseph Smith composed this book, the act was a miracle — keeping awake while he did it was, at any rate..."

I have been on a train without a book and read the train schedule so carefully that I can tell you exactly when the Coast Starlight is supposed to pull into Chemult, Oregon (4:32 p.m.). I have read those Jehovah's Witnesses booklets carefully, having nothing else to read. I have read cereal boxes, marveling at the ingredients I never heard of and did not know existed. I have read and remembered far too many of the names and messages carved into school desks and scrawled on water-closet walls. (That LaQuesha is an *adventuress*.) I have read road signs with such hunger, sitting bookless in the back seat, that I still remember many of the exits off United States Highway 80 in Pennsylvania (Snydersville, Tannersville, Mifflinville, Danville, Reynoldsville, Strattanville, Shippenville, Clintonville, Barkleyville, help me Jesus). I have been on planes without books and so carefully examined the layout of the airports to which your carrier flies that I can find my way through even Ninoy Aquino International Airport in Manila, if need be.

I have occasionally thought that perhaps it all evens out in the cosmic sense, and that every time I find myself bookless and avidly reading the tattered copy of *The Life of L. Ron Hubbard* someone using a *lot* of perfume left on the bus, I am paying for the time I left an Ayn Rand novel in a voting booth, and misadventures like that, of which I am not proud, and have endeavored to confess publicly here, catharsis being the first use of literature. The next step, I suspect, is to vow to change your behavior, so I hereby swear, on a stack of King James Bibles, that I will *never* leave fascist novels anywhere except where they belong.

A Note on
How We Slow Down
Near the End
of a Terrific Book,
Reluctant to Leave
That Wondrous World

Which we all do, of course, I bet every reader has done it ten times at the very least, just off the top of my head I can remember doing it with Robertson Davies' extraordinary *Deptford Trilogy*, and with most of J.K. Rowling's books, and with Thomas Pynchon's masterpiece *V.*, and...well, you know what I mean.

What shall we call it, that unconscious slowing-down, which occurs at exactly the same time as you *so* eagerly want to find out what's going to *happen*! that you take the book with you to the water closet, and on errands, and on lunch breaks, and to dental appointments, and to church, where you sit deep in a shadowy corner and pretend to mouth the responses but really knock off thirty pages while seeming to meditate deeply on matters holy and eternal?

Prosepause, storyslowage, readingreluctability, talewaiting — that exquisite sense of deliberately delaying closure, of stretching out the moment, of sipping and savoring and swirling the characters and world and the ambience and milieu around in your heart before they become, inevitably, as they must, past tense, a book you just read; and while there is a great pleasure in rereading a fine book (after letting enough time pass that you half-forget half of it), it is never quite as salty and stunning a pleasure as the first encounter; and that's another pleasure we should talk about over ale, the deep refreshing astonishment of *discovering* a riveting writer or book you never even *heard* of before — that sense of dawning pleasure as you get to page thirty or so and realize o my sainted mama, this is terrific!

This just happened to me with George MacDonald Fraser's Flash-man novels, of which I read the last (*Flashman and the Tiger*) by accident, was so delighted that I sought out other books by Fraser, discovered there were eleven more Flashman novels, and mooed happily at the prospect of a whole summer spent reading books that turned out to be as hilarious, lewd, informative, and masterfully made as the first. The only fly in the ointment, finally, was the discovery recently that Fraser died last winter, just as he was preparing to write a thirteenth Flashman epic, and it would be embarrassing to confess in public that my first thought was absolute annoyance that he was leaving me in the lurch Flashmanwise, rather than sadness at the passing of a fellow holy being, so let's not mention it here.

But we were talking about the way we all slow down at the end of a great book, reluctant to leave the world that was made in those pages, and it seems to me that this impulse is a great and subtle compliment to the writer, and a telling window on what great writers do, which is to create believable galaxies in which real beings grapple with real pain and wonder, miracle and murder; and isn't is fascinating that one of the greatest human pleasures is to be plunged in a pool of prose that you know to be fictive, but holds you with tremendous energy and zest, really and truly rivets your attention, shivers your heart, opens your eyes, teaches you something true about yourself and your fellow holy beings?

Isn't that really, when you think about it, a most amazing thing, that someone like George MacDonald Fraser sits in his room on the

Isle of Man, and spins a tale, and thousands of miles away you open the bright package in which his tale has been caught, and sprint through most of it, elevated and grinning, and then, some fifty pages from the end, find yourself reading more slowly, consciously enjoying the stagecraft and fireworks, itching to find out how Flashman is going to escape disaster this time, but a little sad too that when you come to that last page, and hear the final snick of the plot falling into place, and see that infinitesimal extra brightness of a printed page on which there is no type on the reverse, something that's been so beautifully present is now memorably past? But onward we go into the ocean of stories, knowing full well that there are many thousands of great books we will never even *hear* of in this life…and shouldn't there be a word for that?

The Box Scores

On the first day of October, in the year of Our Lord 2013, my city's daily newspaper, the oldest continuously published newspaper on the West Coast of these United States, issued daily since 1850, before Oregon was even a state, ceased to be delivered daily to its subscribers, who now receive only four papers a week. This was a sensible, if difficult, business decision, having to do with advertising and resources and digital presence, but I am sure I was not the only citizen in Oregon that morning, and on Mondays, Tuesdays, and Thursdays since, to mourn my lost daily delivery of newsprint.

The rattling truck of the deliveryman long before dawn; the way he deftly wrapped the paper in plastic on days of epic downpour; the careful parsing of the paper for various members of the family, sports here and comics there, news to one and business to another; the poor classifieds heading right to the parakeet's cage, where perhaps he read them quietly; the bemused reading-aloud of horoscopes, and thorough reading of ships in port, and ships expected, and cargoes thereof, mostly grain leaving and cars arriving; the way the comics somehow always acquired a patina of jam, while butter illuminated the business section; the snap and flutter of the paper being folded just so, for easier digestion; and most of all, best of all, the box scores.

All sports have their inky spoor and gnomic codes, after the event, and perhaps all sports reward poring over their exquisite numbers, for the stories hidden therein; but above all sports for box scores I rank baseball and basketball, and the very thought of not running a forefinger daily down the boxes, summer and winter, is saddening to me. Baseball's stolen bases, hit-by-pitches, batting averages computed to the infinitesimal thousandth; the innings pitched, pinch-hitters, attendance; the minutes played in basketball, the shooting percentages, the assist totals, the technical fouls; how many hundreds of times did I tell my small sons a game could be understood full well just by reading the minutes-played column, and noting the rebounding and assist totals, far more important than profligate points?

Many times, boys, many times.

And then, when the paterfamilias has read the boxes with care, and marked the most notable numbers in yellow highlighter, and left the paper folded open to the annotated box scores for his sons to find, he would rise from the table, happy in some small huge odd sweet mysterious way, and gird for work, pleased somehow that Jason Kidd had once again posted a classic Jason Kidd 11-11-11 box score, or that Steve Nash had again approached a perfect shooting game from the floor and the free-throw line while stacking up a dozen assists, or that LeBron James once again had come tantalizingly close to the rare glorious quadruple double, or Kobe Bryant had again somehow played a game in which he never once passed to a teammate for a basket, despite 40 minutes on the floor; and then on the way to work, pondering the glory of box scores, I am reminded of the classic Dennis Rodman box score, which would be something like zero points on zero shots, but 25 rebounds and 5 blocked shots and 4 steals and 2 technical fouls and 1 intergalactic press conference afterwards; but then I remember that the box score, that lovely tiny poem in the daily paper, is no more, at least in Oregon; but then I remember that at least my sons spent their childhoods with inky fingers, and knew how to read that sweet subtle story, and many times called out the most amazing ones to me, from the table where they sprawled, as I was in the other room donning corporate armor; and perhaps it is this last thing I will miss the most; not so much the box scores, but the way they could be an arithmetic of affection, a code for love.

A Note on Ceasing to Read

Another thing we don't talk about much when it comes to books and reading is how almost all readers finally arrive at one crucial and telling moment, one that changes their reading styles forever after — that instant when you realize you *aren't* going to finish the book you are diligently plowing through, and you don't *have* to finish it, and you *can* fling it off the porch with a sigh of relief, and such flingitude does *not* mean you are an ignoramus, and in fact a book's unfinishability reflects less on the reader than on the writer, even on such otherwise excellent writers as, for example, James Joyce, whose *Dubliners* is taut and perfect and whose *Finnegan's Wake* is, let us admit cheerfully here in public, unreadable muck.

Almost every reader achieves this moment of maturity, it seems to me, and it is a remarkably freeing line to step over — to finally give up on reading all of Aleksandr Solzhenitsyn, and realize happily that now you have *years* more to live, or to finally, after a volume and a half of Marcel Proust, to say politely, "Marcel, you are a wheezing neurotic nut, and I wish you the best, but I'd like to read books where things actually happen," or even to say to the genius Henry James, "Hank, old pup, your infinitesimal gradations of social manners are incredibly boring, and reading your denser novels is like being drilled by a very slow dentist," isn't that a refreshing feeling?

There are, of course, many books in which slogging pays off wonderfully — Gabriel Garcia Marquez's *One Hundred Years of Solitude*, say, or Tolstoy's *War and Peace*, both of which demand maybe a hundred pages of patient muddling before they explode into such vast tremendous stories that you are, at the end, loath to leave their extraordinary worlds; and there are many books, such as Cervantes' *Don Quixote* or Melville's *Moby-Dick*, that are so huge and sprawling and labyrinthine that you are as pleasantly addled at the end as you were at the beginning, which is perhaps why you reread them with joy every few summers; and there are books that are hard to read but riveting and unforgettable, and it would have been a real shame not to have played in their intense game, books like Annie Dillard's *For the Time Being*, or Faulkner's *Absalom, Absalom*, or Tim Winton's *Cloudstreet*, or the greatest Oregon novel there ever was, Ken Kesey's *Sometimes a Great Notion*.

But I return to the great pleasure of ceasing to read, or surrendering, or quitting, whatever you want to call that moment in bed or on the beach, on the bus or in the waiting room of the very slow dentist, when you say to, let us say, Scott Fitzgerald or Martin Amis or even Willa Cather, "Folks, enough and too much, life's too short for you to be in my ear any more," and you close the book with a feeling not of regret but of, in fact, joyous resolve; there is a little glint of pride that you have had the guts to say, even to a genius, nope.

I know only two people who still obsessively finish every book they begin, and in both cases I suspect they are the sort of people who organize the socks and underwear in their drawers by color and manufacturer and country of origin, not that there's anything wrong with that, lots of people are deeply neurotic, it's what made this country great, but I believe most readers are like me, and we pick up books for all sorts of reasons, and hope to be grabbed, startled, snagged, riveted, knocked out, nailed, moved, amazed, absorbed, drawn irresistibly into a tale and a world and a tribe of characters who are completely and utterly real, within the first fifty pages or so, at most a hundred; but after that if you find your interest and energy flagging, and the page grows too heavy to turn, and the book sits dusty on the night-table, near the bottom of that stack we all have, and your attitude has quietly morphed into *maybe I'll finish that when I am moaning sick with the flu*, then the end of that reading experience is nigh, and not even the looming pressure of the book club meeting, or the chance to wow a date, can force you back to it.

It happens to us all, it happens every day, it has happened to me with every single Philip Roth novel I have ever briefly handled, and it just happened to me again recently when I picked up William Styron's *Sophie's Choice*, and settled in with pleasure, because I was awed by his *Confessions of Nat Turner,* and deeply moved by his *Darkness Visible*, and impressed by his short stories, but after ten pages I slowed, and thirty was work, and by page fifty I found myself thinking I really *should* finish this... But the word *should*, as you know, is a death rattle, for we never do what we should do, which is the secret to a great deal of human joy and pain.

In the American way I will conclude by celebrating independence, because the best thing about not finishing books you do not wish to read anymore is the way it frees you to read books you *do* want to read but have not read yet, and books you stumble across, and books that are pressed upon you by cousins and other charlatans, and books on other people's night-stands, and books in the waiting rooms of very slow dentists, and books mentioned in the bibliographies of books you loved, and books lauded in book reviews, and books touted by Oprah, and books with shameless vulgar irresistible covers beaming at you from the windows of bookstores, and books you find in the basement that you were supposed to read in college but didn't actually get around to then, and books newly translated into your first language, and books discovered after the untimely death of an author whose other books you admired, and books that your kids are supposed to read for school but leave carelessly around the house, which is a mistake on their part, for that is how one of my sons did not read Jack London's *White Fang* but I did, which led me happily back to *The Sea-Wolf,* which led me for murky reasons to other writers who lived near oceans, which brought me ultimately to the saltiest of all American writers, the great testy genius Henry Louis Mencken, but even Mencken, great as he was, could not get me to keep reading his *The American Language*, which is said to be a total deathless classic but was so moaningly boring that after thirty pages I slammed it shut and grabbed a beer and a son and ran to the sea, the story from which all stories come.

Tenant Lease Agreement (Addendum)

Tenants and their guests are under no circumstances allowed to read William Burroughs out loud, or mime words or phrases written by same, or screen obscure arty films made from his work, or perform obscure arty skits based on his work, or brandish scissors and pretend to cut up pages of prose and rearrange them in obscurely arty ways like old Billy did while claiming them to be literature which they weren't under any conceivable definition no matter what that brilliant marketer of self and cronies Allen Ginsberg shouted.

If any tenant or his or her guest at any time should have the urge to claim that art in any way shape or form, or supposed art like things dunked in urine or buffalo chips scattered in seemingly artful arrangements, should be supported by any kind of public tax whatsoever, tenant and guest(s) will be subjected to the greatest hits of William Shatner for not less than one hour.

Any tenant who says Richard Brautigan is a great writer without actually ever having read a murky page of Richard Brautigan will be escorted from the premises.

Any tenant who has endured James Joyce's deeply awful book of poetry, *Chamber Music*, and speaks honestly of it gets a free month's rent.

Any tenant who knows Henry David Thoreau's real name at birth gets a free month's rent.

Any tenant who ever laughed at a Stewart Holbrook story, or has read a Stewart Holbrook story, or has even *heard* of the deathless and hilarious Stewart Holbrook, gets a free month's rent.

Any tenant who knows where Holbrook's favorite Portland watering hole, the legendary Erickson's Saloon, used to be, gets a free month's rent.

Any tenant who has ever shaken hands with Ursula K. Le Guin (for which you have to bend down, she's the size of an egret), gets two free beers from the management.

Any tenant who answers *Philip Roth!* when asked the finest American male novelist ever will be penalized one additional month's rent.

Any tenant who can within ten seconds name Saul Bellow's birthplace gets a free month's rent.

Tenants and guests may not under any circumstances use, possess, conceal, cook, steam, shelve, play tennis with, bake, roast, sleep with, caress, sneeze on, pummel others with, eat, bathe with, or clean cats with, the collected works of Jerzy Kosinski.

Tenants may use self-help books and Oprah Winfrey corporate materials in the potting shed only.

All poetry must park in clearly marked spaces reserved for it. No exceptions. Poetry found parked in the spaces reserved for other literature will be ticketed.

Fiction of all sorts, especially the nonfiction of James Frey, must park in the spaces reserved for the center of communal life.

Tenants who are or have been editors of any periodical of any sort, including webzines and fanzines and mimeographed alumni bulletins from your late lamented grade school, get a free month's rent.

Tenants who have *published* haiku after the age of seventeen are penalized one month's rent; tenants who have *written* it but not inflicted it on an unsuspecting world are encouraged by the management to keep on in that vein.

Tenants who are or have been or wanted to be newspaper reporters, editors, circulation managers, printers, designers, cartoonists, subscription managers, delivery managers, advertising managers, advertising salespeople, account representatives, technical support staff, custodial staff, insurance representatives, publishers, and human resource and personnel staff, get a free month's rent. Although whoever said, chirpily, *a newspaper publisher, Grampy!*, at age ten, in answer to your grandfather's question, *so, Herman, what is it you want to be when you grow up*? No one, that's who! Any tenant who did so is penalized one month's rent, and has to park with the poetry.

Banning the Ban on Books

Library staffers at the Catholic university where I work recently opened the library's "cage," a small room on the second floor, and placed the books formerly within its confines onto the shelves of the rest of the library. The cage had for nearly a century contained books on the Catholic Church's *Index Librorum Prohibitorum* (Index of Prohibited Books), the list of banned books that began with an Index of Forbidden Works promulgated by Gelasius in Rome in the year 496.

While most of the books in the room made their way into the rest of the library, one riveted me especially: this was a slim volume titled *Prohibited Books*, which contained notes from the late librarian to himself and his successors on "laws concerning prohibited books," "recommendations for the University Library," "clearly condemned books," and "doubtful or borderline cases" (which were to be housed on reserve shelves, and reviewed annually by a four-professor library board).

While the Christian habit of attempting to regulate the reading of the faithful goes back to the Ephesian converts of Saint Paul, who made bonfires of books they considered superstitious (books valued at "fifty thousand pieces of silver"), the *Index* was the most consistent and longest-lasting censorship effort in Western civilization, and even after its death it deserves to be remembered, if only to salute such diligent and well-intentioned folly.

Folly it was. The final edition of the *Index* featured some 4,000 works, many of them deservedly obscure, but some of them among the greatest prose compositions in history: Michel de Montaigne's *Essais*, Gustave Flaubert's *Madame Bovary*, Victor Hugo's *Les Miserables*, the travel books of Laurence Sterne and Joseph Addison, John Milton's *State Papers*, Daniel Defoe's *History of the Devil*, Edward Gibbon's immense and wonderful *Decline and Fall of the Roman Empire*, and the complete works of Emile Zola, Thomas Hobbes, and David Hume, among others. Some of these, like Addison's *Remarks on Several Parts of Italy*, were banned because of their irreverent portrayal of the Vatican City; others, like Montaigne's essays — from which the modern essay genre takes its form and spirit — were banned because of their dangerous relativism and individualism.

The *Index* did not begin in a purely condemnatory vein. Its first incarnation had three parts: a list of the authentic books of Scripture, a list of recommended readings, and a list of heretical and apocryphal books that the faithful were forbidden to study. The *Index* was a resounding success in its first millennium, since printing hadn't been invented and keeping an eye on the few books in the world wasn't difficult. Gutenberg's neat idea threw the Church into a tizzy, though, and in 1467 Pope Innocent VIII decreed that all new books had to be reviewed by authorities before general issuance. Thus came into being a phrase familiar, perhaps, to many readers: *Imprimatur*, "it may be printed," the permission granted by the local Catholic "ordinary," or highest authority, usually a bishop.

The *Index*, with many other aspects of ancient Catholicism, died at the hands of Catholicism's revolutionary Second Vatican Council, and it cannot be said that it is mourned by many, even among the most conservative Christians. One may admire, at this remove, its paternal intent to protect readers from "immorality" (the very spirit, one suspects, that led to the construction and maintenance of the book-prisons like my university's); but one may also cheerfully excoriate its restriction of freedom, its anti-intellectual stance and tone, its distrust of the sense and discriminatory powers of the faithful, and its employment of an enduring evil, censorship, as a tool to encourage faith, which is the search for love amid evil.

A vibrant, dense, joyous faith of any stripe is one which punctures immorality and bad theology, not flees from it, or locks it away in cages. Evil is beaten not by retreat but by battle; and one of the most powerful tools readers and writers have against evils of all sort, including censorious religious monoliths, is their affection and respect for the word. *Veritas vos liberabit,* as the motto of my university has it — the truth shall set us free. So farewell, *Index Librorum Prohibitorum.* We are glad to see you gone, and pleased to see the cage doors flung open.

The Newspaperness
of Newspapers

Hey, I read the papers, so I am well aware of the precipitous national decline in advertising pages, the plummeting numbers of subscribers, the slumps in circulations, the wailing and sobbing of executives as they kneel and worship the holy internet, burning incense before their glowing computer screens in hopes of attracting the 18-to-35 demographic, but the thoughts occur to me, as I am sure they have occurred to you, that (a) maybe newspapers are not dying but dieting, and will soon emerge from this arduous winnowing period healthier and happier, and (b) has anyone paused here along the groaning road to celebrate the sweet inky newspaperness of newspapers? Do we so take them for granted that we don't see how cool and unique they are, in so many odd and graceful ways?

Such as the way they open like wings or arms, and patiently give us stories, without the nagging and wheedling of television, the drone and yowp of radio, the cold glow of the computer. Or the way they cheerfully fold themselves into squares and rectangles and let us read them any old way any old where. Or the way they are friendly and useful and immediate and neighborly with grocery coupons and police logs and shipping calendars and theater listings and smiling profiles of cops and nurses and fifth-grade teachers and small boys who rescue ducklings from storm drains. Or the way they offer themselves with silent grace as kindling and fishwrap and in-a-pinch giftwrap for birthday presents you forgot to get whatsoever. Or the way they get divvied up on Sunday morning to various members of the family according to interest and obsession, the food section going to the father who fancies himself a chef, the sports section to the small boy addicted to agate type, the comics to a second boy, the news to the intelligent and curious mother, the business section to the grandfather who for some reason checks the price of silver and gold every morning and claims to have a serious interest in how much grain is exported weekly from Oregon to countries under constellations unknown. Or the sheer generosity of information and opinion in the paper, some hundred large pages a day of used cars, used dogs, processed political guff, polished editorial prose, furious and hilarious letters to the editor, crossword puzzles, adoptable children, cartoon strips like Mary Worth that have been running since the dawn of recorded time, stock prices, bond markets, bicycles for sale, fulminations and recriminations, lies from the Legislature, photographs from around the world, used tires, maps and graphs, the misadventures of celebrities, scientific discovery, battalion reunions, funeral arrangements, and what time the Blazers are on — among much else.

Consider for a moment that newspapers are organic and recyclable, do not require electricity, are portable, are redolent, can be read by children, foster literacy, foment community, are useful for lining windows and cedar chests, can be used for school projects having to do with volcanic action in the Cascade Range, are sometimes carried by proud dogs, can be used effectively against wasps, can be thoroughly consumed in twenty minutes (forty on Sunday), and are filled with voices from every class and shape and stripe and color and age and sort of human being, and then maybe you will wonder, as I do, if we take their technology and utility for granted. Beautifully designed to fit human life, delivered magically before dawn to your door, costing something like a penny a page, is there any other medium so thoroughly informative, so unassuming, so much a part of communal life that we don't stop to salute it as much as we should? In the same way that we take cops and teachers for granted, and nurses and mothers, and plumbing and blackberries, and literacy and ballots, and marriage and ministers, I think we mostly ignore the sweet wild gift right under our noses — literally, in the case of newspapers, which spread out beneath our hungry eyes every day like countries we have never even imagined. So this morning, maybe right now, take a moment and contemplate the flutter of ideas in your fingers. A curious and lovely gift, yes?

On the Pleasures of Reading the Port Calendar in the Newspaper

First there is the song of the names of the ships, the *Vishnu* and the *Liubliana*, the *Kali* and the *Kenny*, the *Pyxis* and the *Pharos*, the *Chinook Maiden* and the *Eternal Athena* and the *Star Harmonia*... Then there are the blunt terse working boats, the barges and tugs and grain vessels, the latter filled to the brim with Oregon wheat for Japanese tables, hard red winter wheat, dark northern spring wheat, western white wheat... Then there are the destinations and originations of ships, Mozambique and Nanjing, Indonesia and Iwakuni, Aarhus and New South Wales, and how many of us have the same irresistible boyish urge to keep an atlas within reach, and flip to Indonesia, and get lost for a moment among the wet and redolent islands of the archipelago, the smell of teak and bouganville drifting faintly over the breakfast table, before an exasperated teenaged someone snarls for the ketchup a third time?

And the poem of the headings themselves, *vessels in port, vessels due, to depart*... To Depart! In the dim smoky mist of an Oregon morning, with endless rafts of fir trees poking through the fog across the river, the faint shouting of orders and commands, the letting-go of hawsers and cables, the basso groan of the vast ship leaning into the river, the thrum and hum and thunder of the engines as big as cottages in the nether reaches below, the whirl and whine of instruments and machines, the hammering of men's feet on decks, the startle of a heron veering off the bow, the mewling of gulls circling the stern, the faint shiver and surge of a ship headed to sea...

The boy inside the man dreaming at the breakfast table ("dad? the ketchup? hello? dad?") nods for a moment, and the man snicks grimly back into place, and ponders serious adult ideas like shipping tonnage, and oil spills, and tanker hulls, and dockyard unions, and sea pirates, and military repair contracts, and port authorities, and homeland security, and dirty bombs, and carp with eleven eyes, and how it came to pass that ships the size of Luxembourg can get so far up the Columbia and Willamette rivers, but then he reads the words *Chembulk Barcelona, from Qingdao, China, Berth Five*, and all semblance of maturity dissolves like mist over the river, and once again there is a boy at the table dreaming of islands and languages and masts and mid-ocean waves the size of schoolbuses and birds of every color that ever was.

Inside all of us there are many children, some we used to be, and some made of our deepest dreams, and maybe who we are now sometimes needs what mesmerized us then; so the man at the breakfast table, with his sensible shoes and plastic cards, his cell phone and his pension plan, needs that eager heedless dreamy boy more than he knows, and maybe that boy inside him needs only the slightest invitation, the slimmest opening of windows, to leap out, happy and silly and wild; and there, tucked quietly in the corner of the business section, is the Port Calendar, a glorious window to the wondrous world. Fifty lines, at most, in two lean columns, the type as small and unadorned as a baseball box score — but in those workmanlike sans-serif lines there are oceans vast and wild...

The man passes the ketchup, finally, his son wondering what exactly has gone wrong with the paterfamilias this time; and the man drains his coffee, and distributes the rest of the paper around the table for the woman and the girl who will arrive momentarily, and he girds for work, phone in one pocket and wallet in the other, car keys ready to start the day; but he gently folds the Port Calendar into a tiny square the size of a postage stamp, and tucks it in a pocket, for there will come a moment, today or tomorrow or next week, when he will open it, and read the words *Polar Queen* and Paranagua, Veracruz and Shimonoseki, Busan and Brazil, and he will smell the sea...

A Note on the Similarity of Books to the People Who Read Them

They have faces, of course — covers for what is inside, and so often the cover belies the interior, just as the bright alluring faces of people often hide the seething and confusing stories beneath them.

And they have spines of various strengths and tensile pliability like we do, spines that sag and crack and creak, spines that are wonderfully strong and flexible for a few decades and then invisibly deteriorate and lose their glue; and they have arms, so to speak, a book opened wide very like arms flung open; and their back covers, so dense with explanation and blurb, look very like the hirsute backs of heads; and like people no book is exactly symmetrical, the printing of pages necessarily leaving the edges just slightly awry, as we are always, despite all preparation and presentation, slightly awry, one shoe tied loosely, the beard unevenly trimmed, one eye larger than the other, the spectacles askew, all the bills paid but the one that arrives with a snarl.

Some books as small as a hand, some as fat as a head, some broad as a beam, some very nearly the size of a coffee-table themselves; some faint as a whisper, some old and brittle, their skins leathery, their stitching unraveling; some so fragile that a good sneeze would reduce them to dust; yet the ancient fragile ones are so often the ones with the most dignity and the most remarkable stories inside, just like people.

Some blandly bound but roaring inside, some brightly bound but insipid, some missing pages, some amputated, some excoriated, some burned in piles, the ideas inside too incendiary for the authority of the moment. Some imprisoned for the ideas therein, some confined to cells. Some stolen, some kidnapped, some tumble into rivers and oceans, a few have traveled into space and hovered weightlessly under the patient and uncountable stars.

Some humble, some pompous, some evil, some crammed with inextinguishable joy; some born to delight children, some to poke the powerful, some to pierce the heart. Some have no words at all and some are so wordy as to be unintelligible. Some earnest, some nefarious, some renowned, most obscure. Some advance the universe in extraordinary ways, many distract and delay rather than enthrall or edify. Some filled with lust, some with song, some brave, some craven. Some famous for no reason, others incredibly unsung.

All have layers upon layers and are more subtle than they appear. Most get better the longer and deeper you pursue the story. Some end with a bang, some just slide quietly to a close, all are born in mysterious ways we think we can explain but really we haven't the slightest idea how a wriggle of story wends its way into complex creation.

Some we cannot live without, some we leave after years of struggle, some we cannot comprehend or engage, some we cannot forget. Some we wish to have by our sides always, their familiar faces beaming nearby, their voices warm and wise, their lean spines welcoming your fingers, their very scent a redolent country you itch to visit and are loathe to leave. Yet some we dislike, some we detest, some we set ourselves against with faces like flint; many we ignore too easily, many we will never read, a million we will never know, such being the way of the world.

Some once meant everything and now mean nothing. Some grow quietly in our hearts as the years go by. Some spoke powerfully once and then faded. Some arrive suddenly, stunning and refreshing, from unexpected quarters of the compass, and you know in moments you will be friends for life. Some are dressed in motley and rags but a light shines forth adamant and strong; some are all thunder and no rain; some are wiser than their own words can measure.

All matter in ways great and small, as all house stories, and stories are what we are and how we speak and how we mill mundane into miracle.

We take them so for granted. We think new ones will always be freely born. We see them so often we forget how extraordinary they are; until, once in a while, maybe this morning, we think for a moment what the world would be like without them.

II.
NOTES ON
WRITING

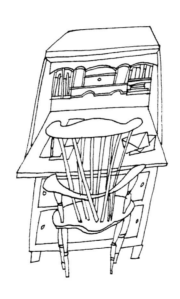

Apostrophism: a Note

My name is Brian, and I am an apostrophist. Unrepentant, unrelenting, and armed with huge honking magic markers in three colors, which I carry with me in the car in a brown bag for emergencies, like recently when I saw a mailbox with THE COONEY'S in big proud letters, and I went back there at dusk, on foot, and deleted the apostrophe, because it's just *wrong*, and someone needs to blow the whistle on this sort of thing, or else we will all be back to wearing leisure suits again, and did that work out for us? It did not.

You could argue that the mailbox belongs to the Cooneys, and so, technically, it is *a* Cooney's mailbox, and you would have a point, but not a very good one, as you well know, because the only other even faintly acceptable option is to reverse the S and the apostrophe, but that entails more work for me, and I have other fish to fry, like getting up on a ladder one of these nights with a can of white paint and painting over that five-foot high E at the end of the word PREMIERE in the phrase OREGON'S PREMIERE AUTO BODY SHOP, a sign in Sherwood that drives me stark raving muttering insane every time I drive past it, as my children can attest, sighing like ancient elephants.

I hear your gentle remonstration: who made you grammar cop of the universe, you pompous idiot? And the answer is, my dad, who initiated me into the inky corps of proofreaders and editors and apostrophists when I was but a pup, meekly holding his hand as he doffed his fedora and pointed out to the village baker that the word BAQERY was illegal and would soon draw the wrath of the intelligence services, and other moments like that, of which there are so many that they flock around me like jackdaws attacking a deacon wearing a coat made of meat.

I remember my dad writing many letters to the town elders until the sign at the end of our block that read YEILD was replaced, and I remember him leaving a copy of *The New York Post* in the confessional booth at church to shrive its many grammatical sins, and I remember him once, on a ferry in New York Harbor, posting me as a sentry at the end of the passageway by the restrooms while he took a bottle of Wite-Out from his pocket and painted out the A in the word WOMAN on the women's restroom door, replacing it with a meticulous E, in pretty much exactly the same typeface. He was a wizard at typefaces, my dad, and, as he says, typefaces are good things to be wizardly about, as you just never know when a typeface emergency will arise, a lesson I have remembered ever since, and often chat about with dad as he plans his corrective adventures. One great thing about retirement, he says, is that you have a lot more time to go around and fix signs like THE LORD IS COMMING, and SALMON FOR SELL, and RUSH LIMBAUGH IS A DOOFUS, which should, of course, read RUSH LIMBAUGH IS A BLOWHARD WHO SHOULD BE SOLD TO SLAVERS IN THE FORMER RHODESIA.

One of my sons, I report with pride, appears to have inherited the clan mania for accuracy, a virtue I discovered in the boy when he was only four years old, and we were poised at the capacious doorstep of a friend's house, and as I nattered away about cabbages and kings and things, I noticed my son attacking the nameplate with a hammer, which he explained later was because it said THE MILLER'S, which was just *wrong*, dad, and if I don't do something about it, who will? This seemed to be an inarguable point, so I didn't argue it, especially as he still had the hammer.

What Writers Think

(All day long) Money money money money money money girls money money money money money money beer money money money money money money money beer *with* girls.

————

(At a reading) How many people are here? Will they buy my book? Does the microphone work? Do I *need* the microphone if only four people show up? Is everyone here related to me? What is everyone leaves during the reading? What if no one wants me to sign a book? What if all these people are here to return my book? What if they throw books at me? Is the microphone big enough to hide behind? Is my fly zipped?

————

(At a reading with other writers) Who goes first? Who's the headliner? Should I go first and get it out of the way and then sit and think about girls and beer or should I pretend to be the main draw? What if these other writers are poets and they drone on incessantly about their gall bladders and previous rafts of husbands? What happens in the question-and-answer period when someone asks a general question and there's that uncomfortable silence as no one wants to be the assertive person who answers first? Should I jump in then and talk about gall bladders? I could tell a joke: there were these three gall bladders in a bar...there was a Catholic bladder, a Jewish bladder, and a Muslim bladder...

(At an awards ceremony) What if I win and have to give a speech and can't get a word out and my gall bladder falls out onto the stage and shimmies off into the orchestra pit? Should I stoop to retrieve it or just let it go where it will? What if I don't win? Do I have to be polite and unassuming or can I stand on my chair and scream imprecations? What if I win and do like Marc Acito did that time, run down the aisle and run up onto the stage and trip on the top step and go flying across the stage into the stunned arms of the mistress of ceremonies? What if I win and get up on the stage and start laughing so hard remembering how Marc Acito flew through the air that my gall bladder falls out?

(Wheedling a publisher) Because this is the greatest book that anyone ever in the history of the universe ever wrote, except for *Always Coming Home* by Ursula Le Guin. Because this book is so much better than a stick in the eye. Because this book is way better than any of the other books that you have published, one of which seemed to be the confessions of a gay heron. Because Ken Kesey is deceased and someone should write wild muddled novels about rain. Because *I* bought the beer today. Because there's a shred of a chance we can persuade Gus Van Sant to make it into a movie because *you* know his aunt's cousin's previous rafts of husbands. Because the market niche for novels written from the point of view of Muslim gall bladders is, shall we say, wide open.

(In the middle of any piece of writing) O my gawd this is drivel. This is the worst muddle ever inflicted on an unsuspecting populace. I should crumple this and go into insurance. I should cease to write forevermore. I should be a pair of ragged claws scuttling across the floors of silent seas. Maybe the Mariners are on. I should eat. Maybe I should take another shower. Who will ever pay for this muck? This is worse than anything Jerzy Kosinski ever wrote, and what could be worse than that? My gall bladder hurts. Just one more cookie. Is that the mailman? How do you spell labyrinthine? Should I do the laundry? Hey, Ichiro tripled!

—·—

(At the beginning of any piece of writing) This is the greatest idea ever! I am a genius! No one ever had this idea before! What a great first line! Being a writer is better than a stick in the eye! This is so exciting! Those words were never in that order in the whole history of the English language! That's incredible! That's astounding! Now what?

Mr Borges

One evening during my sophomore year at Notre Dame I emerged from my dorm room and for once did not wend like an arrow to the Knute Rockne Memorial Gymnasium, where I spent much of my time, nor to the South Dining Hall, where I spent much of my time, nor to any of my mysterious classes, one of which featured a man lecturing mostly in French about paleontology, a class I enjoyed though I spoke neither French nor paleontology, and another of which was a year-long seminar in William Faulkner with five students total, a course in which the five of us kept a surreptitious count of the number of times our professor began a sentence with the phrase *Bill and I...* no, this evening, this soft and redolent Indiana evening, I walked into Washington Hall, a rickety lovely wooden castle, which that evening was to host a writer from Argentina named Jorge Luis Borges. I was not then, at age nineteen, familiar with the work of Mr Borges, but I had accidentally read some of his stories in the library, someone kindly leaving his book open for me on a table and my attention being snagged like a jacket in a door, and I had really liked the way he surfed along the razor edge between fiction and reporting, his scholarly tone somehow making the most amazing pronouncements possible, and I thought I might as well wander over, while he was on campus, and tell him that his work, or what I had read of it, was not bad, not bad at all, which is high praise coming from a teenager, it still seems to me.

Washington Hall then, and perhaps now, was sort of a welter of stairs and doors and odd corners, and as I had never been in the hall before I wasn't totally sure where I was to go to meet Mr Borges, but

I figured there wouldn't be all *that* many people there, I mean, how many people are up to speed on scholarly Argentine fantasists, you know? So I stood by a side door, thinking that probably I would be able to pick Mr Borges out of a group of passersby, and maybe the poor guy would even be on his own, and not know where Washington Hall was, so maybe I could be of use, somehow — an idea that had not occurred to me before, probably ever. So when a small older man in an excellent natty dark suit appeared, accompanied by a helper student with his hand on the older man's elbow, I assumed, correctly, that the dapper older man was Mr Borges, and I said hey, Mr. Borges, how's it going?

Very well, he said, in crisp English, a plus, for I did not speak Argentine.

I read some stories of yours the other day and they were pretty good, Mr. Borges, pretty fine altogether, I said. I thought I would come over and tell you that they were really pretty good. I bet not enough people tell you that they like your stories, if they like them. Sir.

Many thanks, he said, peering up at me, and I realized he was blind. The student who was helping him looked annoyed and sort of seniorish, you know that supercilious look that senior English majors have, like they are *very* soon going to be Major Novelists and you are a slug in the path of their impending glory, and he, the senior helper student, took a step toward the door, looking particularly supercilious, but I sort of liked Mr Borges and didn't see any reason to cut the conversation short, so I held my ground.

Which stories did you like? said Mr Borges.

Well, sir, I don't remember the titles, but there was a tiger on the cover of the book.

Ah, yes, tigers. Remarkable animals. Both alluring and terrifying at once.

That's exactly right, sir. Maybe you should write more about tigers.

The senior helper student pretty much had smoke coming out of his ears at this point for some reason, and he tried to angle me away from the door with his shoulder, but I have brothers so I know from shoulders, and I boxed him out, and told Mr Borges that I too was a writer, and someday I would write books too, and I would send him one or two, if he wanted. He said that would be very kind of me, and then he asked me a question I never forgot.

Why are you a writer? he said, very polite. He was a very courteous guy.

I don't know, sir. I just am. That's what I want to be.

Get as close to the truth as you can, he said, which turned out to be the last thing he said to me, or me to him, because by now the senior helper student, who had been working hard on his footwork behind me, got the drop suddenly, and backed me against the railing, and popped old Mr Borges through the door into the hall before Mr Borges could even get off a parting hey or anything, and I didn't get to say hey or thanks or good luck or anything to him either, which made me feel bad, because he was a really polite and courteous guy, and all in all you would think a blind older guy in a country not his own, accosted by a teenager who has read a few of his stories and cannot remember the titles, would not be quite so courteous, but he was, which I will always remember. Also *get as close to the truth as you can* seems like ever more excellent advice to me, so I share it with you, in memory of Mr Borges. He was a very courteous guy.

A Finger of Speech

...as one of my young sons says at the table one day, superciliously, *that's a finger of speech*, to his twin brother, sneeringly defining a metaphor that just floated by, and away goes dad's brain, sliding right off the table past the ketchup and off into space, where I contemplate the essential accuracy of this remark, for indeed there are fingers of speech, aren't there? The middle finger of speech, used so very often with in many offensive and defiant and enraged manners; and the index finger of speech, indicating primacy or direction, or, if being wagged angrily, denial or disapproval; and the last finger of speech, accusatory or indicatory of prissiness; the left ring finger of speech, indicating marital status; the thumbs up and down of speech, indicating approval, direction, a Tom Robbins cowgirl heroine, or that you would very much appreciate a lift to town; and then there are fingers of speech in endless combinations, such as the thumb and forefinger indicating loserness, the index-and-pinky combo advertising a rabid affection for the University of Texas or gang affiliation (really the same thing), the circled fingers of zero, the circle and ruffled cockscomb that says *okay!*, the number of fingers brandished to number the items under discussion, the flourished forefingers of an Australian Rules football umpire affirming a goal, the forefinger-and-thumb pistols that people point at each other for no good reason, the fingered *v* of victory and peace, the massed ranks of fingers pressed together in prayer and supplication, the ordered ranks of fingers telling motorists to stop, the peremptory forefinger summoning a taxicab, the fingered triad by which we swear fealty and the Boy Scout Oath, the split fingers of the Vulcan salute by which we live long and prosper, the motley parade of fingers playing *here's the church and here's the steeple open the doors and there are the people* to a child agog...

And there are so very many more digitious communications; not to mention the millions of people who speak with their hands in sign languages of endless shapes and sorts, among them interestingly a language called baby sign, by which infants can communicate before they have learned to manipulate their magical tongues to form words with their mouths; and then there are the thousands of infinitesimal gestures and shivers and flutters and flickers of fingers individually and collectively that deliver messages by punch and caress, touch and poke, thump and knuckle; and then there are the eloquent messages of hands at rest, flung or folded, holding a steaming cup, waiting patiently on nervous knees at the doctor's office, patient and still on the tiny chest of a child with a fever; and so we circle back to my sons at the table, boys who were once tiny children with fevers and worse, on whom my hands rested worried a thousand nights and more, but now their hands are fleshy comets and bony boulders, one son insisting on his linguistic prowess and the other insisting he is a doofus and there is no such thing as a finger of speech, *ask dad!*, which they do, and I tell them that they are both right, which as usual does not settle their seething; but I use a forefinger to indicate where they can take their debate, and shuffle off to my desk, and sit down to make a note on the mystery of the matter, my fingers stooping on the story like hawks.

Mr Hillerman

I had the pleasure, some years ago, of having dinner with the late Tony Hillerman, of New Mexico, and that long gentle vernal evening comes back to me now in cheerful memory, for not only was he the most genial and attentive and unarrogant of famous authors, but his wife Marie was even cooler, as is so very often the case with writers of the male persuasion; and some hours of riveting and fascinating conversation passed, in which the Hillermans were astounded by my alluring bride, and we were delighted by the wry genuine honest un-adorned brains of the Hillermans, and as Mr Hillerman said, it was a good thing that he did not have to stand and deliver remarks, for he would much prefer to sit comfortably and have a second beer and continue to talk about books and deserts and the Dineh people of the southwestern United States and his days as a Catholic schoolboy in Oklahoma and his service in the war. He had been an infantryman, he said, a regular old grunt; and it was only some days later that I dis-covered he had won two medals for courage under fire, and a Purple Heart for incurring damages, and that his knees and eye didn't work right because he had been blown up by the Nazis.

He talked about his love for newspapers (he had worked for papers and wire services in Texas and Oklahoma and then been editor of the Santa Fe *New Mexican*). He talked about teaching at the University of New Mexico, which he did for a long time. He and Marie talked with great high glee about their children. He talked about how she was way smarter than he was and she talked about how she had helped him become a novelist by saying *do it* and this was when they had six little kids and hardly a penny.

We talked about how the essay might be the coolest form of all and how he loved writing essays but hardly ever made the time, to his regret, and how novels grow on their own once you have written enough for the characters to take over. We talked about other American writers we admired, most of all Twain and Willa Cather, who if all she ever wrote was *Death Comes for the Archbishop* that would have been masterpieces enough for one writer, said Mr Hillerman.

We talked about how history is stories and research is asking questions about stories and how novels are really collections of stories about the same characters. We talked about how you can always be leaner in your writing and the first rule is indeed slay your darlings. We talked about the Navajo and he said you could spend ten lifetimes listening to stories from the Dineh and never hear but a small percentage of all the Navajo stories there are. We walked about how a lot of writing is just trying to catch and share stories before the stories vanish for one reason or another. We talked about being Catholic and how the deepest way to be Catholic was to not take religion seriously but to take spirituality very seriously indeed. We talked about how writing was spiritual in nature when it was witness, and how witness was really the final gift and responsibility and accomplishment of the writer, if you woke up enough eventually to realize it wasn't all about you.

Right about there Mrs Hillerman said she thought that humility and mercy and kindness were the final frontiers for human beings to achieve, and Mr Hillerman said see, this sort of remark was proof that Marie was smarter than he was, and then we talked about the joy and chaos and hilarity and tension of children, and then, the dinner being at the university where I work, other people began coming over to shake hands and have their photographs taken with Mr Hillerman, and the cheerful intimacy of our dinner ended, but I have never forgotten how unarrogant that man was, how warm and friendly and unadorned, how unimpressed with fame and plaudits, how in love with his wife he was, how happy he was to be himself, unpretentious and unpretending. History will remember the wonderful writer, one of the best to sing the West; but I remember the man who, when I asked him his greatest feat, said, why, asking Marie to marry me!

A Note on
the Misuse of Adverbs

One time my brothers and I were sitting at a balcony table in an ancient pub in New York City, conducting scholarly research, when my brother Thomas overheard a conversation below us and embarked on a memorable adventure that I believe should now be shared with the world, as his prompt and courageous action in the face of what some might call an emergency is something of a lodestar to us all even now, many years later.

We were perhaps ten feet above the floor tables, my brothers and I — high enough for a semblance of privacy, but not so high that you couldn't hear shreds and shards of conversation from the floor. Just below us was a young couple, the woman eager and attractive and the man cocky and fulsome. He was oiling her up at such a rate that finally my brothers and I slowed our conversational ramble and bent to listen. We debated the right word for the young man: *unctuous*, said one brother, *sharkacious*, said another, *oleaginous*, said a third, *horny as Howard Hughes' fingernails*, said a fourth. Finally there was a moment when the young man leaned toward the young woman and gently covered her exquisite digits with his offensive paws and said, *hopefully, you and I...* at which point my brother Thomas stood up suddenly, launched himself over the balcony rail, landed with a stupendous crash on their table, and said to the young man, *Never, and I mean never, begin a sentence with an adverb.*

We had to take up a collection to pay for the table, of course, and we were ejected from the premises, and the young man made a show of glower and threat until my brother Thomas told him gently to stop, but to me and to my brothers, and to my mom and dad when they heard about it, my dad being a newspaperman and my mom a teacher and so the both of them relentless sticklers for good grammar, they were the sort of parents who would instantly correct you when you started a sentence *Tom and me* instead of *Tom and I*, which drove us all insane, but it worked, because even typing the words *Tom and me* here in the prospective context of the beginning of a sentence gives me the willies and makes me expect to hear the polite dagger of my mom's voice from somewhere near my shoulder blades saying *if you say that again I will sell you as a slave to Malaysian pirates*, a sentence my brothers and I heard more than once, and to which one time my brother Tom replied *is that a conditional statement?*, for which he was sent to his room for a week, but anyway, my point was that my brother Tom's quick and decisive action is still a beacon and compass point for us all, and something we should remember when we are daily faced, as we are daily, by the egregious misuse of adverbs.

We need not cower and quaver, we need not flee and wince, we need not resort to long whippy sticks like the nuns used to use with such effect, o how they plied those sticks willy-nilly among the crania of their students, the secret was all in the rolling of the wrist, you just sort of snapped your wrist sharply as if you were throwing a curve, and that thin lathe of ash or willow would flash out and cause wailing and gnashing of teeth, not to mention a welt the size of Utah. One time Sister Rose Marie caught Danny Murphy right in the eye and *his eye fell out!* and rolled under the desks in the third row! but that total suckup Margaret R. Sullivan picked it up right quick and raised her hand and said *here it is, Sister!* in that total suckup voice that melted nuns like butter and Sister stuffed Danny's eye back in his head so fast that *some* kids said it didn't even pop out even though later you could pay Danny a dime to see the dust threads on his eye and how his eye was all discombobulated because Sister didn't have her feet set when she crammed it back in Danny's head, and good footwork is crucial.

Margaret R. Sullivan, boy, that R. drove us nuts, it was bad enough she insisted on writing it whenever she wrote her name on test papers or the chalkboard but *saying* the R. when she said her name, Margaret *RRRRRRR.* Sullivan, like when she was named May Queen and got to say the prayer and started the prayer by saying *I am Margaret R. Sullivan, Queen of the May*, as if we didn't know who she was, well, you wanted to hit her with a long whippy lathe, but you can well imagine why any boy who even approached the holy lathe got lathered with it right quick as punishment for evil ambition, and anyway we got even with Margaret R. Sullivan by teasing her the rest of the year about the *the* there, Queen of *the* May, what did she think May was, a battleship?

In conclusion, the adverb is a crucial and necessary element of the language, and should be respected as such, and used with caution. We do not drive cars without first checking to see if there are enough cigarettes in the glove compartment; why then do we handle adverbs so carelessly, as if they were a resource that could never run dry? So I leave you then not only with a useful story, but with an unforgettable image, one that speaks powerfully and poignantly about the character of Americans, their dash and brio, their verve and grace, and their mordant attention to the rules of grammar. I give you my brother Thomas, one hand on the railing of the balcony, the rest of his long self aloft, his boots pointing grimly toward the smoked salmon salad below, his hair aflutter, his face alight with joy, the moment pregnant with possibility, as all moments are. Such holy battleships, moments; we are granted so many, and sail so few.

A Modest Proposal
for Poetry Inspectors

All male human beings, I suspect, have, when young and stupid, endured a brief infatuation with a girl who thought she was a poet, and so all men have, at some point in their shuffling existences, suffered through poetry readings during which small quiet poets gripped lecterns like the steering wheels of vast ships, explained at incredible length the *circumstances* under which they committed their poems like raving sins, whispered their elephantine incoherent epic, and then, incredibly, *explained* at herculean length how the birds in the poem are actually symbols of revenge, at which point many members of the audience are contemplating the latter, and imagining a world where poets actually do have to get poetic licenses, and swear that they will not suddenly use French phrases in their poems, and vow to never personify favorite body parts of lovers, or write poems in which birds represent anything but birds. Wouldn't that be cool?

Dreaming about that glorious world a little, a world that would require poetic administrative staff, men and women who would design and inflict licensing exams, and take poems out for test drives, and revoke privileges on grounds of obscurity (busted, Wallace Stevens!), and flag down poems that don't meet clean-language standards, I imagine a raft of poetic inspectors, wearing shoulder patches with William Stafford's gnomic smile, and also a whole corps of poetry injectors, cheerful citizens responsible for bracing up the boring — editing traffic signs to add a little wit and lilt, repairing droning political sermons, running retreats for ministers whose homilies have no heft, souping up newsletters, spicing up voters' manuals, and sponsoring an annual Switch Day during which, for example, Walt Curtis enlivens the State Legislature and Ted Kulongoski shouts wild poems on the steps of the Multnomah County Library, Lawson Inada is appointed police chief for 24 hours, and Ursula Le Guin speaks directly by webcamera to every child in every school in Oregon. Wouldn't that be cool?

Think of the advantages of a world with poetry inspectors and injectors: no Hallmark card ditties, lots more Billy Collins, all copies of *Paradise Lost* returned posthaste to England for imprisonment in the Tower, no one pretending to be influenced by Rimbaud ever again, the admirably clear and piercing Wislawa Szymborska an honored guest on Oprah every week, a small sharp poem on the front page of every newspaper every day, the seething youth of America competing hourly for the coolest arrow of a text-messaged poem, Walt Whitman back in the forefront of the litry canon, a President who opens his weekly press conference quoting Linda Pastan or Marie Ponsot or Mary Oliver...

A more musical and rhythmic world, perhaps — certainly a world with more of the electric darts to the heart that great poems can be; for poetry at its very best is the greatest of literary arts (not the greatest of arts, mind you — that would be music, or brewing beer), the one with the most power and passion in the least amount of space, the one that tries most gracefully find the music in the words we swim in, the one that delves deepest into the wild genius of language itself, the one that takes the sounds we make with our mouths and uses them as keys to the deepest recesses of the heart and head.

It is entertaining, at least to grinning essayists, that the price for poetry's occasional unbelievable power is the incredible ocean of self-indulgent, self-absorbed, whinnying, mewling muck produced and published annually under the tattered banner of the Poem; but it is an ancient and useful human truth that every real feat is built on a mountain of failures. For proof consider your short-lived early love affairs, especially the one with the poetess, what was her pen name, Willow? Nighthawk? Kulongoski?

How Did You Become a Writer?

A question asked of me surprisingly often when I visit schools, which I much enjoy not only as part of my overarching subtle devious plan to get on the good side of the children who will soon run the world, but also for the consistent entertainment of their artlessly honest questions (the best ever: *is that your real nose?*), and for the sometimes deeply piercing depth of our conversations; we have suddenly spoken of death and miracles and loss and love, while we were supposed to be talking about writing and literature; and I have wept in front of them, and they have wept in front of me; which seems to me a sweet gift, to be trusted that much.

But in almost every class I am asked how I become a writer, and after I make my usual joke about it being a benign neurosis, as my late friend George Higgins once told me, I usually talk about my dad. My dad was a newspaperman, and still is, at age 92, a man of great grace and patience and dignity, and he taught me immensely valuable lessons. If you wish to be a writer, *write*, he would say. There are people who talk about writing and then there are people who sit down and type. Writing is fast typing. Also you must read like you are starving for ink. Read widely. Read everything. Note how people get their voices and hearts and stories down on the page. Also get a job; eating is a good habit and you will never make enough of a living as a writer to support a family. Be honest with yourself about the size of your gift. Expect no money but be diligent about sending pieces out for publication. All money is gravy. A piece is not finished until it is off your desk and onto an editor's desk. Write hard and then edit yourself hard. Look carefully at your verbs to see if they can be energized. Learn to ask a question and then shut your mouth and listen. Use silence as a journalistic tool; people are uncomfortable with it and will leap to fill the holes, often telling you more than they wanted to. Women especially will do this. Do not misuse this great secret, son. Everyone has sweet sad brave wonderful stories; give them a chance to tell their stories. So many people do not get the chance. Listening is the greatest literary art. Your ears are your best tools. No one is dull or boring. Anyone who thinks so is an idiot. Read the Bible once a year or so, ideally the King James, to be reminded that rhythm and cadence are your friends as a writer. The best writers do not write about themselves but about everyone else. The best writers are great listeners. That is how fiction is hatched. The best fiction is more deeply true than the best nonfiction. Most religious writing is terrible whereas some spiritual writing is stunning. The New Testament in the King James version, for example. Many fine writers do not get credit for the quality of their prose because they were famous for something else: Lincoln, for example. The best writing is witness. The lowest form of writing is mere catharsis. Persuasive writing generally isn't. The finest writers in newspapers are often sports and police reporters. When in doubt about a line or a passage, cut it. All writing can be improved by a judicious editor, except the King James Bible, and even there we could stand to lose some of the Old Book, I think. Don't tell that to your mother. Do not let writing be a special event; let it be a normal part of your day. It *is* normal. We are all storytellers and story-attentive beings. Otherwise we would never be loved or have a country or a religion. You do not need a sabbatical or a grant to write a book. Write a little bit every day. You will be surprised how deep the muck gets at the end of the year, but at that point you can cut out the dull parts, elevate your verbs, delete mere catharsis, celebrate witness, find the right title, and send it off to be published. Do not expect money. Money is gravy. The real reward is to be read; and if you get a letter in response, well, then, you have been paid in the most valuable of coins, the music of another heart. Any questions?

On Dining with the Wonderful Writer Gavan Daws

This was on a beach, on an island so deep in the Pacific that if you set off in a boat from the beach where we ate dinner you could sail south for thousands of miles before you hit a land populated by enormous seals, one of which recently ate a biologist, or conversely you could sail straight north for thousands of miles until you encountered a land where there are enormous bears, one of which recently ate a teenager, but the teenager had been using foul and vituperative language, so you can hardly blame the bear. This was in the same place where another bear wandered into the Royal Canadian Legion Hall and a man who used to be a sergeant told the bear that it would have to leave because it wasn't a member, so it did.

There were a remarkable number of boats moored in the bay where we had dinner, Gavan Daws and me, all sorts of boats, catamarans and outrigger canoes, mostly, but also sloops, and a yacht, and what appeared to be a racing boat, and two rowboats, and a police boat, and a battered green fishing boat with a cabin so tiny you wondered how tiny the actual fisherman, or fisherwoman, was, and I resolved to stay at the table until dawn to see the tiny fisherman, or fisherwoman, but then the wine arrived, and my resolution got distracted, not for the first time. You'd be surprised how easy it is to distract a resolution. You pitch your resolution on a good piece of land, above the water, with a good view of the ocean, and you peg down the corners, and sweep out any and all insects despite their tinny protestations, and kneel your ancient carcass down there in the sand by the door to say your prayers, and then a girl swirls by as supple as a river, or a frigatebird floats over like a gull on steroids, or there's a bottle of wine on the table where there wasn't a *hint* of a bottle a second ago, and suddenly your resolution is scuffling along in bad shoes and mumbling incoherently and looking for beer cans to recycle.

The menu for dinner at the restaurant on the beach offered several thousand choices of fish, there were endless dense pages of fish, the menu was a veritable book of fish, so very many kinds of fish that I lost track of the excellent conversation, which seemed to be about swimming pools and ancient warriors, and I became absorbed by the music of the names of the fish, which included ahi, aku, au, awa, aweoweo, kala, kumu, moano, moilii, oio, ono, uhu, uku, and uu. And then the waiter, who told me he was from Atiu, which means the Island of Birds, explained that many of the fish also had names in my language, names like milkfish and moonfish and goatfish and threadfish and surgeonfish and soldierfish, and this news sent the conversation off the cliff altogether. I made a concerted effort after a while to get back into the game but just then *another* bottle of wine appeared right in front of me, gleaming like a moonfish, and the waiter mentioned that the special was a fish called simply big-eyed fish, a fish that looked exactly like his late uncle, isn't it eerie how that sort of thing happens all the time, and he personally, the waiter, would recommend the special with alacrity and enthusiasm except that it would feel weird to serve up his uncle broiled with a lovely mango sauce, so if we were in agreement he would perhaps point us gently toward some of the many other highlights on the menu, and we agreed to this, as I am sure you would, so that is why Gavan Daws had the moonfish, and so did I.

Mister Burns

At about ten in the morning on my first day as an assistant editor at *U.S. Catholic* magazine, then housed very nearly under the elevated train tracks in downtown Chicago, I was summoned to the august sanctum of the Executive Editor of the Magazine, one Robert E. Burns, known to one and all as Mister Burns. No one knew what the E. stood for although there was a great deal of headlong speculation. Mister Burns wore a lovely burnished silver-gray suit and had the roundest pleasantest ruddiest Irishest face you ever saw until he opened his mouth and said tersely There are several rules here that you ought to know about from your opening moments with us. We do not begin a sentence with the word hopefully. We do not use pointless words like ongoing. We discourage adverbs. We do not conclude pieces in the magazine with cosmic foolery like 'it remains to be seen.' It does *not* remain to be seen. We do not use such foolery as 'on the other hand.' There are no hands in this magazine. We do not edit quotes without that most useful of tools, the ellipsis. We do not respond to lunatic letters with sarcasm or ostensible wit even if they are from John Cardinal Lunatic. The most useful phrase I know is 'you may be right.' We respect authorities of every kind but we do not accept their pronouncements at face value and by the word authorities here yes I do mean Our Holy Mother Church. We do not use other languages in the magazine without a very good reason. Anything that can be said in another language can be said better in American English. There is free coffee in the mail room but you are expected to be reasonable in its consumption. The use of pens, pencils, typewriters, fax machines, reams of paper, and books and periodicals from the library is not monitored by employee but you are expected to be reasonable in their consumption and return the books and periodicals. We will assume by the fact of your employment that you are aware of the history and traditions of Catholicism in America but this is not a historical magazine. We are interested in stories that have something to say about Catholic life in America. We are interested in Catholic life elsewhere in the world but not as interested as we are about Catholic life in America. We are interested in religious and spiritual matters of all sorts but a piece about Hindu life in Australia, for example, would have to be a hell of a fine piece to beat a piece about Catholic life in El Paso, Texas. We expect you to learn to at least grapple with photography, assignment letters, negotiating payment for authors, recruiting authors, discovering and sifting ideas, editing authors whether they like it or not, and contributing occasional pieces of every sort to the magazine yourself in time. However this is not a literary salon and you are not employed to become a writer on company time. You are employed to be an editor at a damned fine Catholic magazine in the United States. What editing actually entails you will have to find out for yourself. Inasmuch as I know and esteem your mother and father, I believe you have a genetic leg up on the task but I have been unpleasantly surprised by genetic collapse before and I am sure it will happen again. Let us hope that I am not speaking presciently about you. In the event that you do turn out to be a decent writer, which is all we can safely hope for on this God's earth, remember that we do not pay extra for contributions to the magazine, and that your contributions to other magazines, which we in general encourage, even for Jesuit magazines, should be composed and polished on your own time and in your own domicile. I believe that covers the general outlines of expectations and responsibilities as you begin with us. I will assume that you have no questions because you are eager to get to your desk and advance the interests of the magazine, an admirable urge. My best wishes on your work. Close the door gently when you leave. If you see an adverb out there kill it. I think that covers everything.

Mr Soisson

The fourth fine editor I worked for — after Mister Burns in Chicago, who taught me that adverbs were lazy and to never start a sentence with the word *hopefully*, and Floyd Kemske in Boston, who taught me to *elevate the reader*, and Ben Birnbaum in Boston, who taught me that if you were going to edit a magazine at all you might as well try to edit the best one in the universe — was John Soisson in Oregon, who taught me to stop thinking of editing as copyediting and rewriting, and start thinking of editing as coaching, provocation, ideas, stimulation, suggestion, listening, and giving writers and artists permission to do the thing they secretly wanted to do but did not imagine anyone wanted to see. A lot of good editing has nothing to do with ink or paper or computers, John taught me. A lot of good editing has to do with dreaming rather than honing; the honing is the last step, not the first. A good editor, I learned, is first and foremost a story-catcher, a story-dreamer, a story-stimulator; a good editor jazzes people to think about what would be great for the magazine, and then he or she picks and chooses from among many lovely works, mixing and matching and honing so as to make a product that sings, while gently placating the poor souls whose work did not make the team — this issue anyway.

Also John made me realize for the first time that there are lots of *kinds* of editors, not just one. There are coaches, who suggest and propose but do not assign or dictate. There are machinists and carpenters, who are superb repairmen of broken and clogged prose. There are genius excerpters, who are eerily able to see the shining nuggets amid the bedraggled dross. There are visionaries and charismatics, whose gift is to draw money and attention and goodwill to the enterprise. There are gifted managers, who are able to easily draw the best from those who labor for them without overmuch snarl and shriek. There are meticulomaniacs whose eye for typographical and grammatical errors and muddled captions and missing credit lines and obtuse subheads, outtakes, rubrics, summaries, abstracts, and other minutia verges on the paranormal. There are punctuation junkies and masters of the absolutely brilliant accompanying art that is neither illustration nor stand-alone glory. There are financial wizards and inky souls granted the subtle gift of ably wheedling the finest contributors without a hint of proper recompense for their contributions. There are those who ably negotiate the brambles and thickets of office and corporate politics, defending and protecting their journals against the teeming hordes of penny-pinchers and sales-chipmunks.

And it was John who taught me the lesson I had dimly begun to learn under Ben Birnbaum; that a magazine was an incredible and unique chance to move readers, to actually reach hungrily for their hearts and souls as well as their brains and wallets, and that a magazine that did not try to connect that deeply with its readers was only information, which is in no short supply, and indeed is today a tide. And this: that a magazine that *did* reach for its readers where they most deeply lived, that *did* occasionally move them and make them laugh and weep and rage and pray, was a magazine that became indispensable to its readers, that became an Occasion on arrival, that was read instantly and thoroughly; and this was not only good business, drawing money and attention and goodwill to the magazine and whatever its sponsoring entity, but also, in a real sense, was good and substantive and rewarding work that served to, ever so gently, and admittedly mostly infinitesimally, bring people together in rich and subtle ways; which is the most you could ever ask for in a profession, an occupation, a vocation, isn't that so?

On Noticing a Man
Reading My Sprawling Novel
on a Train

On the train the other day I saw a man reading *my* novel — the novel I spent five years writing madly and wildly and hilariously and dreamily, the novel I worked on every morning for one delicious and luxurious hour, the novel that I so wanted to be unlike any novel ever written before by anyone in the whole history of people typing fast. And, gaping at the man reading my novel in seat 3B, I had nine conflicting urges all at once. I wanted to leap up and grab him by the ears and ask him if he loved it. I wanted to call everyone else's attention to this amazing sight. I wanted to grin and introduce myself as the poor soul who committed the novel like an inky sin. I wanted to kiss his bald spot for having the literary taste and discernment to read me. I wanted to see what page he was on. I wanted to see if he had underlined or highlighted passages and if he had turned down the corners of pages. I wanted to see if he was smiling or weeping or laughing or sneering. I wanted to see if he had scribbled his name on the title page which would be an ever-so-subtle sign that he wished to keep the book rather than shuffle it along to a remote niece or leave it in the seat pocket. I wanted to see if it was perhaps already inscribed by the author, perhaps to his mother, who sold it online for a small profit.

But I also wanted to look away and leave the man to his work, because more and more I am learning that when your book is pub-

lished, your ship has sailed; your book ceases to be yours the moment
it enters a single reader's head, and what you thought, dreamed, in-
tuited, discovered, and were rattled by, in the making of it, becomes
mere opinion, however informed your opinion might be. This is
startling but riveting, I find; and I discover that not only do I not
mind when people tell me what my book is about — often not at all
what I thought it might be about — but I am often deeply moved and
touched by its effects on heads and hearts, effects I never envisioned
or set out to achieve. This is continuously stunning and mysterious
to me.

On the one side, the sheer comedy of readers telling me what
my novel is about is refreshing: I have been informed that my book
is brooding with death, that it is obsessed with breasts, that is filled
with wheelchairs, that it is an elegy to James Joyce, and that it is a
metaphor for the United States of America, none of which had occurred to me as I wrote it, or afterwards, for that matter. I have also
been informed that the crow at the center of the story is a symbol of
death and God, and I was recently told by a reader that the crow was
obviously a feathered version of the wise fool in *King Lear* — this by a
woman at a book club who also informed me that each of the other
characters in the book was a modern American version of characters
from Shakespeare. She showed me the chart she had drawn up with
inks of different colors, which was a lovely chart, I have to say. I admired it for a while as she advised me to try to be a little more subtle
about borrowing characters from other writers in the future.

But more thrilling than the comedy, more gratifying than the
most lovely rave review, are the ways that what I imagined, what I
typed, bloom and shiver in readers' imaginations. I have had people
tell me my book gave them hope to go on through difficult times. I
have had people tell me my book sang to them when they despaired
of ever hearing music again. I have had a young man tell me mine
was not only the best book he ever read but the book that made him
want to go to college to find out what other sorts of wild shimmering

books there might be for him to discover. *Your book was a door, sir,* he said to me, which is not a sentence I ever heard before, and will be one of the sentences I remember all the rest of my days.

If you are lucky as a writer, and your book achieves a certain popularity and word of mouth, you are asked to do lots of readings, and visit lots of book clubs, and be a visiting writer at colleges and universities, and be the centerpiece of city-reads and even county-reads programs, and this has all happened to me in the last two years. Sure, I am thrilled; I have as healthy an ego as the next guy, and I have kids to feed and cram into college, and after experiencing very little of this sort of inky attention with my first ten books, to be slathered by it now is a kick. But increasingly what I love best about people reading my book isn't the good that comes to me — the heartfelt compliments, the genuine pleasure in thanking me for the odd experience, the small coin of royalties and fees. It's what the story does to its readers. In a real sense, it seems to me, the story isn't mine anymore; when someone reads it, it becomes theirs, and when I visit their local bookstore or library, I am only checking in on a friend, and listening carefully to visions and confessions, not accepting applause for a brainchild.

Sitting on the train, seeing the man across the way reading my novel, I realized again that it isn't my novel any more, in exactly the same way that your brilliant funny complex idiosyncratic daughter doesn't belong to you. You helped make her; you poured incredible effort and imagination into shaping her; you fussed endlessly over her substance and details, to give her the very best chance to leap into the world, to be and bring her best self like an arrow against the dark. But when she *does* leap, when she leaves home and opens herself to the affection and respect and regard and love of others, she becomes her truest self, she becomes a part of those who are entranced by her, who take her into their hearts, who are changed by her music. I keep thinking that I should be a little sad, as my novel and my daughter sail into the hearts of others, necessarily leaving their progenitor behind; but I find that I am not sad at all, but moved so deeply by the sweet wild effect they have on others that I cannot, try as I might, find very good words for what I feel. How ironic; perhaps I should commit a novel on the subject...

Playfulnessness: a Note

Thesis: the essay is the widest fattest most generous open glorious honest endlessly expandable form of committing prose not only because it cheerfully steals and hones all the other tools and talents of all other forms of art, and not only because it is admirably and brilliantly closest to not only the speaking voice but the maundering shambling shuffling nutty wandering salty singing voices in our heads, but because it is the most playful of forms, liable to hilarity and free association and startlement, without the filters and mannered disguises and stiff dignity of fiction and poetry and journalism, respectively.

Discuss.

———

Let me give you an example right off the bat. Just riffing for a moment with the typewriter, borrowing a small son and dragooning him into burbling over this way and banging with one finger, we get ffff and rrrr and bmbmbm, which immediately sound jazzy to me, and send me off thinking about the gleaming glimmering horns in the velvet dark of the jazz club in New York that my sister took me into when I was a teenager, and thinking about the jazzy phonemes my kids started off language with when they were little and spent a lot of time humming consonantal bursts and vowelacious arias, and thinking about how maybe typewriters remember what you type with them, maybe they actually steer you in certain directions for their own devious entertainment, and this sets me thinking about my dad teaching me to type with two furious fingers on his old tall black steel typewriter, and the sheaves of love poems he typed to my mom in blazing dripping afternoons in Manila just before he was sure he was about to die in the invasion of Japan. So here, in the space of two minutes, we have leapt from jazz to jazzy infants to intelligent typewriters to a lanky young sergeant hammering words onto infinitesimally thin sheets of onion-skin paper as parakeets and bulbuls yammered outside in the dense heat, words he thought for sure would be his last, words he desperately wanted to get down before he never saw the girl with the hair to her waist and that irresistible overbite ever again. I mean, there, in two minutes, are a whole bunch of essay starts. Is there any other form that can go so fast and piercingly and honestly and nattily, cutting holes in your heart along the way?

Naaaah.

———

Or here's another example. My grandfather John Francis Clancey, who was raised in Hell's Kitchen in New York City, not far from where we sit today, had a heart attack on the train one day, and I always wanted to try to write about that, and I tried to write it as fiction, but fiction was too mannered and arty and remote for me somehow, so finally I tried to write it like it really and truly happened, and I couldn't write it as straight reportage because it sounded too flat and confessional, but thank God Plutarch invented the essay, because I could come at it in an essay, like this:

"...a savage raging pain explodes in his chest so suddenly and cruelly that it knocks him to his knees and only by shooting his arms out blindly and landing on his hands does he avoid smashing his face on the floor o god o god he he thinks faintly from far far away he can't breathe uh uh uh uh uh uh gasping uh uh uh uh but desperately raggedly he gains a half a breath uh uh uh and gulping uh uh a whole one uh uh then another uh and greedily aah he fills aaah his lungs as deeply as he can aaaah he would eat all the air in the world if he could aaaaah he would suck it dry the blessed air aaaaah and somehow the friendly air aaaaah forces the fire in his chest down aaahh and the rage retreats snarling aaaaah and he kneels there aaaah breathing aaah his shoulders shaking aah his knees throbbing ah his sweat dripping freely to the floor ah his mind whispering o god o god o god..."

You see what I mean? The essay gets there on the express train, you know? I mean, fiction can get there too, but there's always a polite conductor standing there with fiction; the gatekeeper, the man you cannot ignore, the guy who whispers *this is all made up*, remember that, even as the very best fiction, while invented, is utterly true. It's a puzzle, eh?

———

The essay is a jackdaw, a magpie, a raven. It picks up everything and uses it. It borrows everything and bends everything to its nefarious porpoises. The quick sketch of character and moodiness and evocativeness and action of fiction, the musicality and cadence and swing and rhythm and crisp imagery and line-cracking power of poetry, the play and banter and battle of voices of the theater, the camera eye of film, the shapeliness of sculpture (I always wanted to write an essay about weight that would actually get skinnier as you went along, with occasional binges where it bulges out again, wouldn't that be cool?)(or an essay about mountains that parades up and down alpinically, or an essay about caribou migration, say, that goes along for fifty pages but only two inches high, or an essay about windows with windows in it, seems to me you have a bigger playing field physically with essays than you do with poems), the athleticism and grace of dance, all these things are meat for the essayist — and the essay because of its form and size lends itself more to playfulness in terms of speed and pace and timing than other written forms — poems are bursts (and really, if we are being honest, all long poems, especially book-length poems, don't really work as *poems*, do they? they're just too...looooooong, you know? I mean, who really thinks of the Odyssey or the Illiad or God help us all that incredibly boring prison sentence called *Paradise Lost* as a Poem?), plays and novels and nonfiction books are long. *Songs* are playful — think of Joe Cocker's 'You Can Keep Your Hat On' — but songs, when you think about it, are two art forms married to each other. Which is why music with lyrics is perhaps the greatest art form of all, seems to me; but of written art, I think essays are the coolest widest broadest biggest form. Everything fits in the essay, and it's nearly naked.

———

Right about here scholarly-type people will say yeah, well, got any examples, got any documentation, got any illustrations? And being a happy student of the glory of the essay in the greatest of hands I say sweet Jesus yes, think of Natalie Ginzburg's chant and cadence and swing, the tennis match of her great essay "He and I" — "He is hot and I am cold. He loves libraries and I hate them. He loves travelling. I would like to stay at home all the time..." She steals litany and music from poetry. Or think of Robert Louis Stevenson's glorious furious "Open Letter to the Reverend Doctor Hyde," the blunt terse judicial accusatory tone — you you you — echoes of the courtroom speech, the case for the prosecution — and then it flies up and away into an extraordinary prayer at the end, one of the greatest closing passages in the history of essays, bless his soul, that poor man, dead at forty-four. He crams fury and spiritual genius into what seems for a while like straight reportage or notes from a deposition and makes it dance, yes? Or the genius Annie Dillard, with her broken-whiskey-glass-and-ten-packs-of-cigarettes-day voice, in her extraordinary essay "Living Like Weasels," which begins like any old "nature essay" (man, what a reductive and thus dismissive term that is) about paying attention to that which we hardly pay any real attention to (this being the subject of all essays, really), and suddenly goes *flying into the brain and soul of the weasel*, o my god o sweet jesus wow. Doesn't she steal the imaginative fire of the best fiction, in a hundredth of the space, and make a dart to the heart?

———

And, you know, not to be rude or anything, and not to try to start a fire, but just to try to gently say, hey, are we totally sure the emperor is wearing his undies today, isn't one of the great virtues of the essay that it's short? I mean, with total respect for doorstop novels, and muscular nonfiction epics like Peter Matthiessen's *The Snow Leopard* or Jan Morris' brilliant Pax Brittanica trilogy, isn't short almost always better than long? I hear everyone gasping with horror, but c'mon, let's be honest, isn't an arrow better than a tank when it comes to hitting hearts and heads? And isn't hitting hearts and heads the point? And isn't using the arrow that might hit the most hearts quickest perhaps the best idea? So if lots and lots of people will read a brief talkative odd funny pointed cheerful testy voice talking at them from a page, or a screen, or a radio, or whatever cool toy our children will invent next, but not so many people will spend a week with a really big book, or try to decipher a poem, or endure the dental work that is an awful lot of journalism, or see through the glittering neurotic screen that is so much short fiction, well, doesn't that mean perhaps that the essay is the form with the most pop and verve and connective electricity? Could that be? Could it be that we are gathered at what today is actually team meeting for the form that could maybe most change the universe as we know it? Could it be that maybe I am right for a change, and for once am not a complete and utter doofus and bonehead?

———

And a last note about shapeliness. If we grant for a moment that I am right that essays are glorious because they are for the most part unfiltered, and so a direct and unadorned and naked form, which is good; and we grant also that the essay is the closest form to the human voice, which is good, because we listen to easily and naturally to voices, and don't have to strain and labor and work and digest, we just dig the voice, as we were trained to do since even before we were born; and if we grant also that the essay is particularly cool because it's short and direct and a dagger and a dart rather than an epic or labor or doorstop or something you really are going to get around to next summer when you have time which you won't — that still leaves that nagging question that I get all the time from smart-ass high-school sophomores, what's the difference between an article and an essay? Hey, Mister, all these cool things you say about essays, don't they apply to articles in the best hands, articles written by great story-catchers and storytellers like Mike Royko and Murray Kempton and Dexter Filkins and Anna Quindlen and the late great Molly Ivins? To which I say, well, yes, except that journalism in general has to stay on a road, has to have an aura of information, has to at least pretend to be reasonable, whereas essays run anywhere they like; and essays, I would maintain, are also shapelier, more attentive to beginning and middle and end, more attuned to the ways and means by which we tell stories. Essays maybe are a little more carpentered, you know? and more liable to be more vehicles for discovery rather than mere knowledge. Think how many times in your own work you were typing along happily, cursing and humming, and suddenly you wrote something you didn't know you felt so powerfully, and maybe you cried right there by the old typewriter, and marveled, not always happily, at what dark threads your typing had pulled from the mysterious fabric of your heart. Maybe that happens the most with essays. This could be.

———

To return to the original thesis: the essay is the most playful and coolest form because it is the most naked. It is without much artifice, in the end; only enough to build a lean-to on the page for the reader and the writer to live in, for a few minutes. It is not a song by the fire, as poetry is, as poetry was certainly born as; it is a not a vast house in which are many mansions, as novels and other prose tomes are; it is not the terse ostensibly neutral (or neutered) reportage that journalism is, or the casual shaggy gossipy confessional that a letter is as its best; nor is it a song, a rant, a note, a blog, a speech (although a great speech is sometimes eerily close to a great essay, yes?), and along with all that it is not, it is not usually disguised or mannered in any way. As a general rule the essay is a clap on the back, a hand outstretched to be grasped, a blunt voice in your ear. Every other genre has some filter, some jacket it wears, some attitude it is supposed to have, some definition that hovers around it like a nimbus, but not the essay; the only definition that applies to the essay is that it be an adventure, a walk in the woods, a idea pushed and prodded and poked and played with. If an essay leans too much toward the scholarly, it becomes a doddering avuncular article; too far over toward mere parade of facts, and it smells like journalism; too stern and instructive and scoldacious, and it morphs into lecture and sermon and homily; too spitting mad and uncontrolled and it is a rant, or Ann Coulter's diary; too uncontrolled and wandering and it is perhaps a blog entry, a letter, notes for an essay to be made. Direct and unadorned, for the most part — that is the essay. No frills, no filters, no manners, no capering motley, not much ego, it is not only closest to the speaking voice, which is why I love it so, but perhaps closest to the inner voice we all have in the deepest chambers of our hearts. Maybe that is why it is finally such a powerful form, the essay; not because it's closest to us, but because it *is* us.

No

The most honest rejection letter I ever received for a piece of writing was from *Oregon Coast Magazine*, to which I had sent a piece that was half bucolic travelogue and half blistering attack on the tendencies of hamlets along the coast to seek the ugliest and most lurid neon signage for their bumper-car emporia, myrtlewood lawn-ornament shops, used-car lots, auto-wrecking concerns, terracotta nightmares, and sad moist flyblown restaurants.

"Thanks for your submission," came the handwritten reply from the managing editor. "But if we published it we would be sued by half our advertisers."

This was a straightforward remark and I admire it, partly for its honesty, a rare shout in a world of whispers, and partly because I have, in thirty years as a writer and editor, become a close student of the rejection note. The shape, the color, the prose, the tone, the subtext, the speed or lack thereof with which it arrives, even the typeface or scrawl used to stomp gently on the writer's heart — of these things I sing.

One of the very best: a rejection note sent by the writer Stefan Merken to an editor who had rejected one of his short stories. "Please forgive me for not accepting your rejection letter," wrote Merken. "At this time I cannot accept a rejection of my short story. I accept more than 99 percent of the rejections I receive. Many I don't agree with, but I realize that accepting a piece of fiction for publication is a very subjective judgment call. My acceptance of your rejection letter is also a subjective process and therefore I am returning your letter to you. I did read your letter. I read every letter I receive. Your letter was well-written, but due to time constraints from my own writing schedule, I am unable to make editorial comments. I do make mistakes. Don't you, as an editor, be disheartened by this role reversal. The road of publishing is long and tedious. You need successful publications and I need for successful publications to print my stories. I will expect to see my story in your next publication. Good luck in the future."

——•——

The range and scope are astonishing. I have twice received two-page rejection letters from magazines, one an epic and courageous deconstruction of my essay and its many flaws and few virtues, and the other an adventure in sophistry that I still marvel at, in the way you admire a deft bank robber from afar — such astounding creativity, turned to such empty enterprise. In the early days of my own career as an editor I took rejecting pieces very seriously, and tried, as much as possible, to write a thoughtful note explaining why the piece was not quite something for me to accept and pay for. But as all new editors learn, such earnest letters from editors very often are taken by writers as invitations to amend and resubmit pieces, or worse, to argue and debate, and most editors come round eventually to terse generalities simply to defend their working hours and shreds of sanity. Plus I learned that debating poets in particular was painful, although it did give me the chance to daydream about a series of rejection notes designed specifically for poems, which would fault rhythm, meter, cadence, swing, image, line-breaks, verb choice, elusiveness, allusiveness, self-indulgence, self-absorption, liability to lust, and too much muck about love. I nearly had the card printed up that way, with little boxes you could check, like Edmund Wilson's famous **EDMUND WILSON REGRETS THAT HE CANNOT...**, or the lovely form letter that Ursula Le Guin sends to this day, but I got sidetracked by a torrent of devotional poetry that I had to reject post-haste, and never got around to it.

Many magazines lean on a form letter, a printed note, a card, and I study them happily. *The New Yorker*, under the gentle and peculiar William Shawn, sent a gentle yellow slip of paper with the magazine's logo and a couple of gentle sentences saying, gently, no. Under the brisker Robert Gottlieb, the magazine sent a similar note, this one courteously mentioning the "evident quality" of your submission even as the submission is declined. *Harper's* and *The Atlantic* lean on the traditional Thank You But, *Grand Street* among other sniffy literary quarterlies icily declines to read your submission if it has not been solicited, *The Sun* responds some months later with a long friendly note from the editor in which he mentions that he is not accepting your piece even as he vigorously commends the writing of it, *The Nation* thanks you for thinking of *The Nation*, and *The Virginia Quarterly Review* sends, or used to send, a lovely engraved card which is worth the price of rejection. The only rejection notice I keep in plain view is that one, for the clean lines of its limbs and the grace with which it delivers its blow to the groin.

I am no poet, as friends of mine who are poets are quick to remind me, darkly, but here and there I have inflicted poems on various and sundry small quarterlies, and I have come to love the bristle and bustle with which they reject work. I mean, it takes brass balls, as my brothers say, to reject a batch of poems with a curt note while including a *subscription form to the review in the same envelope in which the rejection huddles.* You have to admire the defiant energy there, the passion for persistence. The sheer relentless drive of the small to stay alive is more remarkable, in the end, than the grandeur of the great, no?

Sometimes I daydream of having rejection slips made up for all sorts of things in life, like for moments when I sense a silly argument brewing with my lovely and mysterious spouse, and instead of foolishly trying to lay out my sensible points which have been skewed or miscommunicated, I simply hold up a card (**BRIAN DOYLE REGRETS THAT HE IS UNABLE TO PURSUE THIS MATTER**), or for when my children ask me to drive them half a block to the park (**NO WAY**), or when I am invited to a meeting at work I know will drone and moan for hours (**I WOULD PREFER TO HAVE MY SPLEEN REMOVED WITH A BUTTER KNIFE**), or for overpious sermons (**GET A GRIP!**), for oleagenous politicians and other mountebanks (**IF YOU TELL ONE MORE LIE I WILL COME UP THERE AND PUMMEL YOU WITH A MAMMAL**), and etc.

On the other hand, what if my lovely and mysterious spouse issued me a rejection slip on the wind-whipped afternoon when I knelt, creaky even then, on a high hill over the wine-dark sea, and stammered *would would would will will will you you marry me*? What if she had leaned down (well, not quite leaned down, she's the size of a heron) and handed me a lovely engraved card that said **WE REGRET TO INFORM YOU THAT WE CANNOT ACCEPT YOUR PROPOSAL, DESPITE ITS OBVIOUS MERITS**? But she didn't. She did say *yeah*, or I thought she said yeah, the wind was really blowing, and then she slapped her forehead and went off on a long monologue about how she couldn't *believe* she said yeah when she wanted to say yes, her mom had always warned her that if she kept saying yeah instead of yes there would come a day when she would say yeah instead of yes and really regret it, and indeed this very day had come to pass, one of those rare moments when your mom was exactly right and prescient, which I often think my mom was when she said to me darkly many years ago *I hope you have kids exactly like you*, the ancient Irish curse. Anyway there I was on my knees for a while, wondering if my lovely and mysterious paramour had actually said yes, while she railed and wailed into the wind, and finally I said, um, is that an affirmative? because my knees are killing me here, and she said, clearly, yes.

I suppose the whole concept of the editorial Yes is properly the bailiwick of another essay altogether, but I cannot help pondering the positive for a moment, for there are so very many ways to say yes, more than there are to say no, which is interesting on a philosophical and cultural level as well as an editorial one. You can say yes with glee and astonishment, you can say yes with the proviso that you anticipate changing this bit or that, you can say yes while also saying we'll need to sail toward one more draft, you can say yes to a piece of the piece, you can say yes to the idea but not to the piece, or you can, in a sense, say yes to the writer but not to the piece — this isn't quite for us, but we're interested in the verve and bone of your work, call me. The best advice for saying yes I've heard came from a friend of mine who edits a nature magazine. *Use the phone,* he says. *It matters that a voice says yes.* This is the same guy who says you should always envision a writer as your mom when you say no, so as to avoid being snotty, and that you should overpay a young writer on principle once a year, just to mess with the universe.

My friend James and I have for years now plotted a vast essay about editing, an essay we may never write because we have children and paramours and jobs and books to write, but we take great glee in sketching it out, because there are hundreds of subtle joys and crimes of editing, and editing is hardly ever what the non-inky world thinks it is, which is copyediting, which is merely the very last and easiest piece of editing — rather like a crossword puzzle, something you can do near-naked and beer in hand. *Real* editing means staying in touch with lots of writers, and poking them on a fairly regular basis about what they are writing and reading and thinking and obsessing about and what they have always wanted to write but haven't, and also it means sending brief friendly notes to lots of writers you have never worked with yet in hopes that you will, and also it means listening to lots and lots of people about lots and lots of ideas, some or all of which might wend their way into your pages, and it means being hip to the zeitgeist enough to mostly ignore it, and it means reading your brains out, and it means always having your antennae up for what you might excerpt or borrow or steal, and it means tinkering with pieces of writing to make them lean and taut and clear, and always having a small room open in the back of your head where you mix and match pieces so see if they have any zest or magnetism together, and it means developing a third eye for cool paintings and photographs and drawings and sculptures and carvings that might elevate your pages, and writing captions and credits and titles and subheads and contents pages, and negotiating with and calming the publisher, and fawning at the feet of the mailing manager, and wheedling assistants and associates, and paying essayists more than poets on principle, and soliciting letters to the editor, and avoiding conferences and seminars, and sending the printer excellent bottles of wine on every holiday, including Ramadan and Kwanzaa, just in case.

And dickering with photographers, battling in general on behalf of the serial comma, making a stand on behalf of saddle-stitching against the evil tide of perfect-bound publications, halving the number of witticisms in any piece of prose, reading galleys backwards to catch any stupid line breaks or egregious typos, battling on behalf of the semicolon, throwing away all business cards that say **PROFESSIONAL WRITER**, trying to read over-the-transom submissions within a week of their arrival, deleting the word *unique* on general principle and sending anonymous hate mail to anyone who writes the words *fairly unique*, snarling at writers who write *We must* or *We should* or, God help us all, the word *shan't*, searching with mounting desperation for a scrap or shard or snippet of humor in this bruised and blessed world, reminding male writers that it's okay to acknowledge that there are other people on the planet, halving the number of times any writer says *me* or *I*, checking page numbers maniacally, throwing away cover letters, checking the budget twice a day, and trying to read not most but all of your direct competitors, on the off-chance that there might be something delicious to steal.

And then away to lunch.

———

My friend James has a lovely phrase for the joy of actually editing a piece: mechanic's delight, he calls it, and I know whereof he speaks, for I have sipped of that cup with a deep and inarticulate pleasure. I have been down in the engine room of very fine writers' minds, my fingers following the snick and slide of their ideas into sentences. I have worked like hercules to clean and repair a flawed piece and bring out the song fenced round by muddle. I have distilled vast wanderings into brief journeys. I have snarled with delight to discover a writer deliberately leaving a fat paragraph for me to cut, a gift he confessed with a grin. I have said no to the great when they were fulsome and yes to the unknown when they were stunning. Many times I have said yes when I should have said no, for all sorts of reasons, some of them good, and more times than I know I said no when I should have said yes.

———

I have rejected essays but turned them into letters to the editor. I have rejected essays but asked to borrow one or two of their paragraphs for class notes in the back of my magazine. I have rejected essays but recommended submission to another magazine, which is a polite service to the writer, but I have also rejected essays and inflicted the submission on another magazine, which is a venial sin. I have rejected essays by pleading space concerns, which is not always a lie. I have rejected essays I admired for inchoate reasons that can only be caught in the tiny thimble of the word *fit*, about which another essay could be written. *It doesn't quite fit*, could there be any wider and blanker phrase in the language, a phrase that fits all sorts of things?

I was lucky to train under wonderful and testy editors, a long brawling line of them, starting with my dad, who edited a small trade newspaper, laying it out in the basement of our house with redolent rubber cement and long strips of galleys and galley shears the size of your head. He was and is a man of immense dignity and kindness, and no editor or writer ever had a better first editor than my dad, to whom I would show my early awful overwritten overlyrical self-absorbed stories, which he would read slowly and carefully, and then hand them back, saying gently *beginning, middle, end.* I thought he was going nuts early, the old man, but he was telling me, in his gentle way, that my pieces were shallow, and that no amount of lovely prose matters unless it tells a tale — a lesson I have tried to remember daily since.

On my first day as an editor, in Chicago many years ago, beneath the roar and rattle of the elevated train, the first great editor I worked for gave me a gnomic speech about how *we do not use the word hopefully to begin a sentence here*, another remark I never forgot. Later, in Boston, I worked for a very good editor whose mantra was *elevate the reader*, and then I worked, again in Boston, for a genius editor who actually had a bottle of whiskey in his desk and a green eyeshade in his office. He cursed beautifully, in great rushes and torrents, and wrote like a roaring angel, and had been in a rabbinical seminary, and had shoveled shit in an Australian circus, and driven a cab in Brooklyn, and much else. As testy and generous a man as I ever met, and a glorious editor, whose driving theme was *say something real, write true things, cut to the chase.* More advice I have not forgotten (hopefully).

Some of the best yesses I have issued over the years: yes to a sixty-year-old minister in Texas who had never published an essay in his life or even sent one to an editor but he finally wrote down (very slowly, he told me later) a brief piece about the two times in his life, many years apart, a Voice spoke to him out of the air clear as a bell and to his eternal credit he did not in the essay try to explain or comment on these speakings for which refusal to opine I would have kissed him, given the chance. Yes to a twenty-year-old woman who wrote a lean perfect piece about her job running the ancient wooden-horse carousel in a shopping mall. Yes to a sixty-year-old woman who wrote the greatest two-line poem I have ever seen to date. Yes to a quiet Mormon man the age of Christ who wrote an absolutely haunting essay about laughter (which was also funny). Yes to a twenty-year-old woman who was a waitress in a bar in a rotten part of town and wrote a haunting brief piece about the quiet people who sat at the bar every night when it closed. Yes to a sixty-year-old man who drives a bus and wrote a piece about a six-year-old girl who was so broken and so hilarious and so brave that when I finished reading the essay I put my face in my hands and wept. Yes to a fifty-year-old doctor who had sent me arch essay after arch essay but finally sent me a perfect essay about the best teacher she ever had, to which I said yes so fast I nearly broke a finger. Yes to half of an essay by Andre Dubus, an essay we were cheerfully arguing about when he died of a heart attack, and I asked his oldest son if I could print the good half and not the mediocre half, and he said yes, which made me smile, for I could hear Andre cursing at me happily from the afterworld, in that dark amused growly drawly rumble he had when alive.

—·—

When my own essays are rejected I immediately inflict them on another editor, whereas I am always mindful of my dad's advice that a piece isn't really finished unless it is off your desk and onto another's, and I am that lesser species of writer who can never stay focused on One Important Project but always has four or five pieces bubbling at once, so my writing life is a sort of juggling act, with pieces flying here and there, some slumping home through the mailbox and others sailing sprightly away in their Sunday best, eager and open-faced. When one slouches home, weary and dusty, I spruce him up and pop him into the mail and lose track until either he comes home again riddled with arrows or I get a postcard from another desk, sometimes in another country, *I've found a home!*

And then every few years I gather some thirty or forty together again, actually printing them out and spreading them out on the floor, a motley reunion, so as to make a collection of essays, and I have often thought that there is an essay even in this small odd act, their jostling for position, my kneeling over them attentively, worrying again about their health, listening to their changed and seasoned voices, listening for who wants to stand by whom, putting them in parade order like kindergartners bounding off on a field trip, two by two like braces of birds. No one ever talks about the paternal aspect of being a writer, the sending of your children off into the world, where they make their own way, go to work, enter homes, end up in the beds of strangers, and only occasionally do I hear news from the frontier. But such is the wage of age.

Why *do* editors say no, anyway? Well, I cannot, of course, speak for All Editors, and I cannot even properly speak for myself, because I reject some pieces from a murky inarticulate intuitive conviction that they're just not our speed, but there are some general truths to note. We say no because we don't print that sort of material. We say no because the topic is too far afield. We say no because we have printed eleven pieces of just that sort in the past year alone. We say no because the writing is poor, muddled, shallow, shrill, incoherent, solipsistic, or insane. We say no because we have once before dealt with the writer and still shiver to remember the agony which we swore to high heaven on stacks of squirrel skulls never to experience again come hell or high water. We say no sometimes because we have said yes too much and there are more than twenty pieces in the hopper and none of them will see the light of day for months and the last of the ones waiting may be in the hopper for more than two years, which will lead to wailing and the gnashing of teeth. We say no because if we published it we would be sued by half our advertisers. We say no because we know full well that this is one of the publisher's two howling bugaboos, the other one being restoring American currency to the silver standard. We say no because we are grumpy and have not slept properly and are having dense and complex bladder problems. We say no because our daughters came home yesterday with Mohawk haircuts and boyfriends named Slash. We say no because Britney Spears has sold more records worldwide than Bruce Springsteen. We say no for more reasons than we know.

—·—

Even now, after nearly thirty years as an editor, years during which I have rejected thousands of essays and articles and poems and profiles and ideas (even once a play, *I have rejected a play*, there's the phrase of the day), I still, even now, often feel a little sadness when I say no. Not always — I feel nothing but cold professionalism when I reject a submission from someone who clearly hasn't the slightest idea or interest in the magazine itself, and is just using the magazine as a generic target for his or her work; for example people who submit fiction, which we have never published — or never published knowingly, let's say.

But far more often the writer *has* looked at the magazine, and is submitting something we might publish, and *did* make it with all his or her heart, and it just doesn't make it over the amorphous and inexplicable bar set in my head, and I decline their work with a twinge of regret, for I would so like to say yes, to reward their labor and creativity, the way in which they have opened their hearts and souls, the courage they have shown in bleeding on the page and sending it to a man they do not know, for judgment, for acceptance, for rejection. So very often I find myself admiring grace and effort and craftsmanship, honesty and skill, piercing and penetrating work, even as I turn to my computer to type a rejection note, or reach for one of our own print-ed rejection slips, to scrawl something encouraging atop my illegible signature. So very many people working so very hard to connect, and here I am, slamming doors day after day.

———·———

After lo these many years as a magazine editor I have settled on a single flat sentence for my own use ("Thanks for letting me read your work, but it's not quite right for this magazine," a sentence I have come to love for the vast country of *not quite right,* into which you could cram an awful lot of sins), but I still have enduring affection for the creative no, such as this gem sent to a writer by a Chinese publication: "We have read your manuscript with boundless delight, and if we were to publish your paper, it would be impossible for us to publish any work of a lower standard. And, as it is unthinkable that in the next 1,000 years we shall see its equal, we are, to our regret, compelled to return your divine composition and beg you a thousand times to overlook our short sight and timidity."

I have been an editor for thirty years, and in those dark and inky years during which my eyesight has gone and my fingertips have been hammered into blunt squares, my patience evaporated and my posture shot to hell, I have never seen, given, or received anything to top that as a rejection notice, and so I conclude as once did that noted editor Henry Louis Mencken, of Baltimore, who once finished a harangue aimed at newspaper editors (whom he called "a gang of pecksniffs") by noting that "no one has asked me for my views, and moreover, my experience in the past has not convinced me that they are desired. So perhaps I had better shut up and sit down," which I do.

Mr Dubus

He died in winter, his heart failing him at home on a hill above the Merrimack River, and his death in 1999, at age 62, robbed this nation of its finest Catholic writer. No one since Flannery O'Connor wrote with such grace and honesty of the power of faith in American lives, and I believe that no one in America ever wrote with such sinewy beauty of the sacrament of every moment and the stunning simple daily miracle of the Eucharist. We can savor, with pleasure and respect, the work that Andre Dubus left behind at his early death — a novel, eight collections of stories, two extraordinary collections of essays — but we mourn the silence of a man who portrayed, as no one before or since, the struggles and joys of Catholic faith woven through American life.

There have been, and are, wonderful tellers of that tale: O'Connor, J.F. Powers, Thomas Merton, and Walker Percy among those deceased; Annie Dillard, Barry Lopez, James Carroll, and Paul Wilkes among those living. Powers' tales of rectory and monastery life are classics, but of fiction writers who have tried to show the heroic and haunted struggle for grace in daily life, I believe O'Connor and Dubus stand clear against the rest, and Dubus, like O'Connor, was also a deft and passionate essayist in later life.

Dubus's own life fell into two great watersheds: before and after the night of July 23, 1986. Before that hot night on a highway he was a writer known for his stories of people under pressure, admired for the honesty of his stories, the way they looked gently and respectfully at the lives of the poor, the tired, the troubled, especially in the tougher sections of the declining mill towns along Massachusetts'

Merrimack River valley. Before that night he'd been a captain in the Marines, a Louisiana boy who'd arrived finally in New England to be a college teacher. He'd been married twice, blessed with five children, had another child on the way; but then came that night on a highway.

Driving home, he stopped to help a young couple whose car had hit an abandoned motorcycle. As he helped them to the shoulder of the highway, a speeding car barrelled into them, but Dubus — in an instant reaction he attributed to his Marine training — yanked the woman out of the way. She was injured only slightly, but the young man was killed, and Dubus's legs were smashed beyond repair. For the next 13 years he lived in a wheelchair, and in that chair he conducted a brave and tender and difficult search for both the grace to live his own new life and ever more direct ways to write about courage under duress. And more and more he wrote about sacraments, about the miracle of every moment, about the grace of God he felt and tasted and savored everywhere he spun in his chair.

"A sacrament is physical, and within it is God's love," he wrote, "as a sandwich is physical, and nutritious and pleasurable, and within it is love, if someone makes it for you and gives it to you with love; even harried or tired or impatient love, but with love's direction and concern, love's again and again wavering and distorted focus on goodness; then God's love too is in the sandwich. On Tuesdays when I make lunches for my girls, I focus on this: the sandwiches are sacraments. Not the miracle of transubstantiation, but certainly parallel with it, moving in the same direction. If I could give my children my body to eat, again and again without losing it, my body like the loaves and fishes going endlessly into mouths and stomachs, I would do it..."

Catholicism, perhaps more than any other faith, is story — the ocean of Jewish stories that provide context for the Messiah, the riveting stories Jesus told, the stories of Jesus' life, the stories of the millions of people who have believed in the Son of Light since he walked Judea, the stories we tell every day in the Mass, the stories we teach our children so that they too might yearn for and pursue light in darkness, grace amid brokenness. And Catholicism is paradox; it is the relentless belief, against horrible hourly evidence, that divine love made and sustains and graces the world and will do so unto the end. And Catholicism is rich in ritual and symbol, in characters and miracles and magic. No wonder that the faith lends itself easily to stories — Flannery O'Connor's fanatic believers, Powers' calculating priests, Dubus's open-hearted yet rock-ribbed accounts of sacraments everywhere and in everyone.

A great American storyteller died in winter, six children lost their father, and Andre's town was reduced by an inimitable one; and the day that Andre had a heart attack and died on his hill near the Merrimack River, Catholics in this nation lost one of their most articulate and sharp-eyed brothers, a burly bearded man whose smile was nearly as big as his heart. His gifts were many, his courage in pain admirable, his grace an education. May he rest in peace in the palm of the Mercy.

Novelizing

Having discovered (late) the peculiar pleasures of writing novels, I have happily been committing novels one after another in recent years. For various foolish reasons I had to take a break recently from the novel I have been utterly absorbed in every morning for months, and when I returned to it finally the other day I discovered the characters were annoyed with me, and were initially recalcitrant to speak, as if they were on strike; finally I realized that they were hurt that I had abandoned them, that I had left them to their own devices. I could not very well explain about contracts and travel delays to them, but after a while things warmed up and we got back to work, with only minor grumbling.

But this made me stop and think about the odd dynamic of making novels. They take a long time to make, and you do not get paid while making them, which is awkward when the dental and tuition bills come. You do not know quite what you are doing or what is happening while you are making them, and can only hope for the best; in my experience, if you try to command and control the characters, they lose their verve, and become mere puppets, and the whole thing loses its energy and dash and rich mystery. You write a lot of stuff that seems cool and lyrical and amazing and then you have to cut it because it does not serve the story. You wander off on tangents and spend too much time with the wrong characters, just like you did in life when you were young. You leave gnomic hints for yourself in the text and then forget utterly what that was all about. You have the constant urge to suddenly write in Gaelic or blank verse, which you must repress. You have the terrible urge to bury red herrings and private jokes in the text, which you must repress. You have the constant urge to allow buses to speak, and herons to pontificate, and horses to mate with postboxes, which you must repress.

Finally when the novel is done you must show it to the one reader you trust most in this world, and hope she says *o my god* rather than *that's nice*, and then you must resist the urge to show it to friends, who would only issue advice, and then you must seek out a brilliant soul or sucker to publish the novel, and even if and when it is published, you must keep your dreams real, and not tell everyone Brad Pitt will be starring in the movie, and hope that the book sells more than one copy to one person per week.

In my limited experience, though, by the time the novel is loose in the world, with a shiny cover and cheerful blurbs and heated marketing rhetoric that I helpfully supply, I am utterly absorbed in another novel, and can only watch those characters from afar, with affection and a sort of reverence; they came to me, they presented themselves, they graced me and my fingertips for a year, and now they are launched on their own, in their papery ship and electric download, and I feel for them as I feel for my children: proud of who they became, thrilled at their independence, and more than a little sad that our time living together is done. But on we go.

Writing Oregon

I was at book club recently, as the grinning guest whose novel was the subject of discussion, when I was asked who were the finest writers and books in the long history of Oregon, and yet again fulsome garrulous wholly debatable opinion rose in me like sap, and out poured a headlong speech of such remarkably subjective nature, albeit informed by much reading and a great deal of chat with Oregon readers and writers, that it seems entertaining to reproduce some of it here.

To answer the first question: In no order, Ken Kesey, Ursula Le Guin, Barry Lopez, Beverly Cleary, and Stewart Holbrook — the last of whom was the funniest and most headlong and colorful of them all, and is now almost forgotten, which is a shame, because his *Holy Old Mackinaw* (a cheerful history of American logging) is a masterpiece.

To answer the second question: Kesey's *two* masterpieces, *Sometimes a Great Notion* and *One Flew Over the Cuckoo's Nest* — the latter arguably the better, more coherent book, but the former a sprawling epic thing that all Oregon writers, I notice, agree is the best Oregon novel of all. The *Lathe of Heaven*, by LeGuin. *The Brothers K* and *My Story as Told by Water* by the terrific David James Duncan. *The Country Boy*, by Homer Davenport, a hilarious memoir entertainingly illustrated by himself. Lopez's *Winter Count*. Sallie Tisdale's *Stepping Westward*. *Hole in the Sky*, by William Kittredge, a searing memoir of his youth on the high dry side of Oregon. *True Believer*, by Virginia Euwer Wolff, and *Ramona the Pest*, by Beverly Cleary. *The Nez Perce and the Opening of the Northwest*, by Alvin Josephy, a brilliant historian who earned a Bronze Star as a Marine in World War II. *Voyage of a Summer Sun* by Robin Cody, who canoed from the source of the Columbia River to its mouth, which took him one whole summer. *Fire at Eden's Gate: Tom McCall and the Oregon Story*, by Brent Walth, a great biography of our best governor. *The Jump-Off Creek*, by Molly Gloss, the best novelist in the state today. *Riverwalking*, by Kathleen Dean Moore, the best essayist in the state today. *Every War Has Two Losers*, by William Stafford, who was not only Oregon's poet laureate but America's, and not only wrote some 60 books of poems but was a brilliant asker of questions about the foul calculus of war; for all that we sing and celebrate the poet this year, his centennial, it's the question-asker I most admire, and would inflict on every citizen in the state, if I could; not to mention this sweet wild silly glorious selfish violent brave nation of ours.

On Renaming
Almost Everything
in the Known Universe

Here's an idea: how about if all the cars and trucks and sports teams we name for fleet and powerful animals and cosmic energies and cool-sounding things that don't actually exist or mean anything (Integra! Camry!) are, effective immediately, renamed for literary characters and authors? Wouldn't that be cool? So instead of the Escalade we have the Evangeline, instead of the El Dorado we have the Elmer Gantry, instead of the Hummer we have the massive gleaming Huckleberry Finn. And it's even more fun with sports teams — the Portland Trail Babbitts! The Detroit Twains! Imagine the logo possibilities — the Twains with a bushy-haired Samuel Langhorn Clemens peering cheerfully over the bill of their ball caps, the University of Georgia's Fighting Flannery O'Connors with that wise bespectacled young soul on their broad chests, the mind doth reel.

And this allows us to beautifully sidestep the contentious problem of sports teams being named for people with skin slightly darker than most of the people playing and following that team — Redskins, Braves, Chiefs, Indians, it's a particularly dopey custom, and we are easily rid of it when we find ourselves rooting for the Cleveland Icaruses and the Kansas City Chinos (with the overture from West Side Story blaring from every speaker in the stadium).

For once city council and corporate board meetings would be riveting, wouldn't they, as Los Angeles teams vie to see who can snag the names Marlowe and Chandler, and who will be the Los Angeles Easy Rawlins? The New Orleans Moviegoers, the Boston Dennis Lehanes, the Harvard University Fighting Henry Adamses...

Just the loss of so many utterly weird and puzzling car names would be a great gift to the known world. Achieva, Cabrio, Elantra, Galant, Impreza, Passat, Reatta, Vandura, all gone and unmourned, and in their places we find the Deerslayer, the Scarlet Letter, and the Augie March — although there are some current cars that could and should keep their names: the Somerset and the Swift, for two, not to mention Stanzas and Dashers and Darts.

I can hear you arguing now: isn't it an act of wild creation *itself*, to invent ridiculous names for cars, names that sound sort of cool and dashing and fast if you don't think about it at all, but as soon as you think about it for a second you start laughing so hard your sprain your eye, and then you laugh harder imagining the eager devious souls who had to sell those names to the startled high priests of marketing, who many times incredibly must have said yes! yes! when someone said how about Camargue or Justy or Nubira, chief, which now I have to stop thinking about that moment in Detroit because my eye hurts? And to answer your question, yes.

Anyway I personally think this is an excellent idea, because it leads to hours of happy dreaming about the University of Massachusetts Moby-Dicks, or the University of Oregon Randall Patrick McMurphys, who play at the aptly named Mac Court, or the Toronto Robertson Davies, on which team every player is asked to sport the enormous glowing beard of the salty soul for whom the team is named. Such speculations, I find, are perfect for wasting the hours that a responsible man would be looking after the laundry and the parakeets, but this line of thinking brings me right to the late William Wharton, who would have smiled widely, I bet, if the Baltimore Orioles renamed themselves the Birdys in his honor, which they haven't yet. But they might.

A Bogey Tale

Jeykll and Hyde came to Robert Louis Stevenson in a dream, in October 1885, on a wind-whipped night by the sea. He'd fallen asleep uneasily, remembered his wife Fanny, and in the night "my husband's cries caused me to rouse him, much to his indignation. 'I was dreaming a fine bogey tale,' he said reproachfully," and he told her what he had dreamed — the essence of the book he would write twice in the next six days, all the while confined to bed and hardly able to speak for fear of his lungs hemorrhaging.

He woke at dawn and wrote furiously. At lunchtime he came downstairs "preoccupied," remembered his stepson Lloyd, "hurried through his meal, and announced that he was having great success with the story, and was not to be interrupted even if the house caught fire." Two days passed, Stevenson scribbling furiously in bed. On the third day he came downstairs with the manuscript — 30,000 words. He read it aloud to Fanny and Lloyd by the fire.

Lloyd listened, "spellbound, and waiting for my mother's burst of enthusiasm," but it did not come: "Her praise was constrained, the words seemed to come with difficulty; and then all at once she broke out with criticism. He had missed the point, she said; had missed the allegory; had made it merely a story — a magnificent bit of sensation-alism — when it should have been a masterpiece."

Stevenson was livid, enraged, "his voice bitter and challenging in a fury of resentment," said Lloyd, 17 years old at the time and frightened to see the stepfather he dearly loved "impassioned and outraged." Lloyd fled, Stevenson stomped back upstairs, and Fanny stayed by the fire, "pale and desolate."

Then Stevenson returned. "You're right," he said quietly to Fanny. "I've missed the allegory, which is, after all, the whole point of it." He threw the manuscript in the fire. Fanny and Lloyd shouted and reached for it but Stevenson stayed their hands: "In trying to save some of it, I should have got hopelessly off the track. The only way was to put temptation beyond my reach."

He wrote it again, in three days, and then off it went to be published, as a thin book costing a shilling. It soon became one of the fastest-selling books in history. Today millions of copies have been sold in a hundred languages; and from it have been born dozens of plays, movies, even, God help us all, a musical.

But to me *Jeykll and Hyde* is far more than tale. I think no truer thing about men and women has even been written, for Stevenson captured the most maddening of human truths: we are capable of leering, squirming, unimaginable evil even as we are capable of astounding and incredible grace. We court and slay, we rape and heal, we lie and confess, we rant and pray, we rage at the Other even as we know, deep in our uttermost bones, that the Other is also us.

A gaunt Scot dreamed the answer to the final human question long ago: how will we win the war in ourselves? A battle of every hour, in every heart; but the victory begins when we speak the hard truth about the Jeykll in us.

Scribbling & Dribbling:
a Note

In recent years I have become absorbed by the startling basketball pedigrees of many of the Northwest's finest writers — Sherman Alexie and Robin Cody and Barry Lopez were all high school stars, David Duncan was a springloaded rat-ball forward, and even Ken Kesey, for all his fame as a wrestler, is reputed to have been a decent, if foul-prone, hoop player. Taking this line of thought out for a silly walk, I started wondering where other fine writers would fit on basketball teams — the sturdy and sinewy John Daniel, for example, once a logger, is clearly a rooted center, and the tiny and brilliant Ursula Le Guin, deft and inventive and confident, is clearly a point guard. Molly Gloss, willowy and efficient, looks like a smooth forward to me; the effervescent Marc Acito looks like the fizzy wild-eyed guard you want leaping off the bench and energizing a dull game; Tim Egan, with his all-round skill set, can play three positions; Ivan Doig and Tom Robbins, let's say, are guards who check into the game together, the disciplined Doig calming the wildly talented but infinitely combustible Robbins...

The more I did this with Northwest writers for sheer entertainment (Stewart Holbrook distracting the refs and the other team with a string of witty remarks, Beverly Cleary letting dogs romp on the court, Chuck Palahniuk getting into fistfights, Bernard Malamud playing the first quarter and then fleeing to Vermont), the more it seemed to be oddly revelatory of characteristics of their work, and the more I itched to apply the filter to American literature at large. I mean, doesn't it say something about Barry Lopez's eerie control of his prose, its cadenced dignity, that he once controlled the ball and the rhythm of the game? Doesn't it reveal something of Duncan's soaring imaginative leaps as a writer when you realize he was a wild floating egret of a ballplayer?

So I see Saul Bellow, un-tall and burly and cocky, as a point guard, a sort of Jewish Deron Williams; and Ernest Hemingway, all muscles and glower and attitude, as a power forward, a kind of literary Maurice Lucas; and Mark Twain, who did everything well, as a literary Oscar Robertson, dominating smoothly without seeming to expend much energy (ah, the art of artlessness). And off we go, dreaming: John Updike as Kobe Bryant, unbelievably great sometimes but somehow just a tad too solipsistic; and Flannery O'Connor dropping one killer dart after another from the corners, a female Sean Elliott; and John Steinbeck toiling quietly and consistently for years, always excellent and hardly ever dramatic, the Tim Duncan of American letters; and Dave Eggers as Chris Paul, talented and generous, and Annie Dillard as LeBron James, great right from the start and maybe one of the best ever...

We could, of course, play this game endlessly, with writers who were better players than writers, like the late James Carroll, or writers who were good players who later wrote beautifully about the game itself (John McPhee and John Edgar Wideman are probably all alone there), but this line of thinking always depresses me, for basketball, it seems to me, has not produced superb writing, in the way that, say, baseball and golf and cricket and boxing have. You could easily count the classic basketball books on one hand: David Halberstam's *The Breaks of the Game* (which is more about race and money than it is about professional basketball), McPhee's *A Sense of Where You Are* (a paean to Bill Bradley when he was the best college player in the nation in 1965), Terry Pluto's hilarious *Loose Balls* (about the immensely colorful and chaotic American Basketball Association), Darcy Frey's riveting and chilling *The Last Shot*, maybe Pete Axthelm's *The City*

Game, and that's about it — Bill Simmons' *The Book of Basketball* is hilarious once, but no one will ever reread it, and Bob Ryan's *Forty-Eight Minutes* is terrific if you are a Celtics nut, of which there must be a few. After that it's magazine articles blown up into flimsy books (John Feinstein), self-gratifications (Charles Barkley et al), journals of championship years (an endless parade), spiritual silliness (Phil Jackson), or books that seem to be about basketball but aren't, really (Larry Colton's *Counting Coup*). Where is basketball's Roger Angell or A.J. Liebling? Where is the sport's masterpiece of its role in culture, like C.L.R. James did for cricket in *Beyond a Boundary*? Where is the writer who sings it beautifully for decades, so that after a while it's one long sweet story about people and commitment and passion and laughter, as Herbert Warren Wind did for golf?

When younger I daydreamed that that writer might be me, but now I am a cagey veteran, all too aware of the holes in my game. But mark my words: there will come a writer who will make one startling book after another about basketball. It's the most sinuous, quicksilver, flowing, graceful game there is, the most American in its generosity of scoring and gentle violence, and there will arise a writer to match it, I hope...

The Dark Joys
of the Book Review

We skim and scan and peruse them, we note the ones that glow, we grin at those that snarl, but I bet you a pint of excellent ale that no one really thinks of the book review as a genre itself, a shapely form, a unique and peculiar corner of literature; but maybe we should.

Consider the difficulty of composing a brief piece, both graceful and pointed, that must juggle many tasks: assess the feats and flaws of the book at hand, its place in the works of that writer, its place in books on that subject, its general substance or silliness, and — most of all — whether the book is worth cold cash. Additionally a good review should sketch the subject of the book itself in such a way that the reader gets a quick lesson in Antarctic exploration, beekeeping, Guy Fawkes, Tom McCall's fishing waders, etc.; one subtle kick of a book section in a newspaper is that it is fully as informative and stimulating as the rest of the paper (indeed usually more so), whether or not you immediately shuffle to the bookstore to lay your money down.

And it is a form with masters, like John Updike (whose book reviews are literary essays of exquisite grace and erudition, far more interesting and pithy than his novels, with far less neurotic lusty misadventure) or Christopher Hitchens (whose reviews are energetic, opinionated, bristly, tart, and often hilarious essays), or James Wood (who is almost always startlingly perceptive and who, bless his heart, coined the happy phrase 'hysterical realism' to describe much modern fiction). And like any form it has its charlatans and mountebanks;

what is more entertaining, among the dark pleasures of reading a newspaper, than realizing that the reviewer has not actually read the book in question, and is committing fizzy sleight-of-hand? Or reading a review that is utterly self-indulgently about the reviewer, not the book? Or a review that is trying desperately to be polite to a book with as many flaws as the New York Knicks? Or reading a reviewer, like Michiko Kakutani of *The New York Times*, who must spend hours every day sharpening razors with which to eviscerate the books she reviews, and has liked, as far as I remember, only two books in the history of the universe, Ian McEwan's *Saturday* and Richard Flanagan's *Gould's Book of Fish?*

Ah, low humor, a venial sin. Sorry. But there are great gifts in the book section too. Has not every one of us been introduced here to writers and books that subsequently mattered immensely to us? Have we not all heard here snatches of the voices of sage elders like Ursula Le Guin and Peter Matthiessen and Eduardo Galeano? Have we not been reintroduced to men and women of real vision and piercing holiness, like Abraham Lincoln and Flannery O'Connor? Have we not discovered writers and books we might never have encountered in the normal chaos and hubbub of our days — Alan Furst's haunted war novels, David Duncan's spiritual essays, Stewart Holbrook's resurrected loggers and thieves? In one sense the review section is a digest, a distilling, of the vast ocean of books (there are more than a million books published every year, one every thirty seconds, says the Mexican writer Gabriel Zaid) into those that might matter most; and in a nation and culture in which ideas and debate and story still supersede the gun and the lash, we might take a moment to ponder the book review as a quiet inky pillar of the body politic.

There are still more quiet pleasures in the book section. To discover a terrific writer's excitement about other writers, say — Barry Lopez singing William deBuys, Cynthia Ozick celebrating Amos Oz, Margaret Atwood applauding Alice Munro. Or the arrival, with a tremendous splash, of a ridiculously gifted young writer grappling not-quite-smoothly with a capacious talent — a Zadie Smith, a Jonathan Safran Foer. Or meeting a writer of startling grace and power whose stories stitch and braid into your heart — a Helen Garner, a Haruki Murakami. Or meeting again, with a shiver of warm recognition, writers who mattered to you once and who leap right back to the top of that teetering pile of books on your bedside table: Willa Cather, Robert Louis Stevenson, George Orwell, Eudora Welty. Or, another grinning low pleasure, reading a review and recognizing that brassy pub-argument voice, cocksure about writerly rankings — a voice I drift into myself, I confess, when I insist, banging my tankard, that Twain is the greatest of all American writers, and Bellow the greatest of modern ones, and Stevenson the most broadly masterful of all.

It is an odd genre, to be sure, the review, and every bit as chancy as its literary cousins — many times a superb book was panned on first appearance, many times reviewers turn out to be laughably wrong about a book's staying power, many times a very fine writer of something else turns out to be a terrible reviewer, and many times a bad review leads to bickering and wailing — would the letters page of *The New York Times Book Review* be any fun at all without the moaning of offended authors and the icy sniffy replies of reviewers?

In the end the book review seems to me every bit as laudable a form, when in good hands, as film and theater reviews have become when sculpted by such as, say, the hilarious Anthony Lane and the perceptive John Lahr. To sit on Sunday morning and flip open the papery halibut that is *The Oregonian* and peruse the reviews is to be in a village green of voices, learned and light-hearted, erudite and exuberant, snarling and singing. It is to be in a sea of stories. It is to be in conversation, in a real sense; and it seems to me these days that listening attentively to each other, and speaking honestly of that which is foremost in our hearts, is the essential duty of both national and spiritual citizenship. We are ourselves stories, sometimes shapely and sometimes stuttering; and the more we tell and hear stories, the more we trade tales of grace under duress and courage against the dark, then the more we keep reaching for what we are at our best, and remain leery of arrogance, and remember that there are many roads to light.

So why, if well-made book reviews are so important, do such lowly ink-stained wretches as me attempt them? Well, you get to keep the book you review, which is pretty cool, and you get to scribble in it, which is *really* cool, but most of all for the simplest reason of all — books are fun, and poking into new books is more fun, and discovering and celebrating great books is the most fun. It's the reverse of that feeling we have all had as readers, of slowing down as you approach the end of a great book, because you're reluctant to leave that world you can only enter for the first time once; the grail for reviewers is the dawning realization that the book in your hand is extraordinary, something that matters, something that will hit hearts. Now *that's* cool.

Auto Correct: a Note

Recently a Rigorous Peer-Reviewed Academic Journal Not to Be Named Here accepted a small headlong essay of mine, and the elephantine process since then has been entertaining — a series of incredibly intricate maneuvers, all accompanied with the most amazing stern tart commanding cover notes. This morning's note, for example, says "Please check that the author surnames have been correctly identified by a pink background... Occasionally, the distinction between surnames and forenames can be ambiguous... Please also check all author affiliations..."

This sent me into immediate reverie, of course, and I will happily spend an hour tonight in Auto Correct, just for fun... "The author's surname is of course a fiction adopted seven generations ago to survive under the cruel and murderous English empire under which Dubhghaill, Gaelic for dark stranger, was changed by imperial fiat to Doyle...choice of surnames is referred to editor as something of a moral dilemma; if we use the Anglicized one, does that not entail support for murderous regimes, and utter disrespect for aboriginal peoples? As regards forename, author has been called Brian, Brain, Byron, Bryan, Beak, BD, B, Hey You (by grandmother not sure which small crewcut grandson he was; there were a lot to choose from) Idiot, Liar, Meathead, Self-Absorbed Buffoon (former girlfriends), Buster, Bud, Yo, and Freak-Flag (New York City policemen), etc. Also family legend has it that had I been born female I would have been named Virginia, for reasons that elude me and send my dad into hysterics, so in the spirit of respecting all genders and possible permutations of same, choice of forename referred to editor; if you choose the male forename, does that indicate marginalization of the feminine in all of us? And let us not even tiptoe into the affiliations problem. Does that count Boy Scouts, from which I was ejected (politely)? The Catholic Church, bless its motley chaos? The Saint John Vianney Seventh Grade Boys Basketball Team? The Fellowship of Christian Athletes, to which I belonged for half an hour, until I discovered there was no beer as promised? Boston, where I loved for many happy years but now do not? The worldwide community of Jewish men — do I belong to that if I was once dragooned into attending a *bris* with my brother because a Jewish friend of ours could only scrape up eight Jewish males and he made us stand in, which my brother and I remember for our outright and outspoken horror at what then happened to the poor defenseless baby? Do I still count as a Knick fan if I stopped liking the Knicks in 1974 and now detest them with a deep and abiding detestation? I refer these and further questions if necessary to the editor...

Selling Stories

I remember the moment I realized I was not a journalist but a sales and marketing man. This was in Boston, many years ago. It was March, the muddiest month. At the time I worked for an excellent Catholic university, hammering away at stories for the alumni magazine, and I thought of myself as a writer, a collector of tales, a portraitist in prose, something of a minor inky artist, but one slushy afternoon, as I thrummed my keyboard, it suddenly came to me that I was in advertising — that I was promoting a product, soliciting attention for it so as to recruit purchase, inviting investment, establishing brand identity and affiliation, doing my utmost to lure cash into the coffers of the corporation.

I stopped typing and sat there gaping. For twenty years, since I'd been a boy of ten aping my newspaperman father and learning to type fast while cracking wise, I had dreamed of being a journalist, working for a magazine, walking in the footsteps of E.B. White and A.J. Liebling and S.L. Clemens, smelling and shaping stories, off-handedly gathering my essays into ballyhooed books, wandering the highways and byways of this bruised and blessed land, charming and chaffing testy editors, singing and celebrating the grace and humor and idiocies of the Americans, such a glorious and foolish race; but there I was, on a sleeting afternoon on the edge of the city, a sales-man. I had so wanted to be William Faulkner, and at age thirty I was Willy Loman.

And yet, and yet, I began to think, what *was* the product? Wasn't it epiphany and opportunity, opening and elevation? Wasn't I selling an ocean of new chances, or at least the *chance* at those chances? Wasn't it a village of stunning ideas and shivering moments? Wasn't it the electricity of an awakened mind and a startled soul? Wasn't I, in fact, selling, to young men and women and the parents who loved those children with all their humming hearts, the possibility of finding a riveting self they had never even imagined?

And the product itself, I realized, was delightfully ephemeral, it could not be touched or tasted, boxed or regulated, it was a verb of a product, remarkably different for each consumer, an experience, an emotional country; it was not a shoe, a truck, a plastic disk stamped with labyrinthine code, it was not even a service, a tour, an expedition complete with guides and goblets. It was, simply, An Education, something that some would explore to the deepest caverns of their souls and others would breeze through beerily, and no one, not even the all-powerful vice president for student affairs, could dictate its shape for each student.

This cheered me up wonderfully, and I began to realize too that I was a crucial actor in the play, a critical cog, for if no one told stories of what it was like to be educated there, of the salt and spice of that intellectual and cultural and spiritual and social village, soon no one would enter it, and it would wither and die, reduced to shreds of memory and acres of archives, yet another college that used to be, alive only in anecdote, not in the tumultuous hearts of teenagers, the furnaces of the future. The stories there swam in the air by the millions, every student and professor and staffer and alumnus and alumna and parent and neighbor and donor had a hundred, and without story farmers like me to cull and harvest them, to mill them into meals for the curious world, there was, in a sense, no college at all, for if we have no stories we have nothing; that being the cruelty of diseases that rob memories and leave only the fruitless body yearning for its salty spirit.

Twenty years later I still sell stories, though now I have graduated to a Holy Cross university, from which height I tease my Jesuit friends about their admirable order being banned by the Vatican for forty years. But all the rest of my days I will remember that moment when I first saw what I was, and what it meant; and I have been singing ever since.

Shoshana

I have had the inordinate luck, in 30 years as a writer and editor, of meeting and conversing and corresponding with many of the finest writers of our time; was there ale enough between us, I could tell you entertaining stories of Peter Matthiessen (who once spent an hour regaling me with his experiences in the Navy in Hawaii during the Second World War, when he ran the military baseball league), and Barry Lopez (a genius, and one of the wittiest men I ever met), and Ivan Doig (who loves to talk about the craft of writing, the linguistic carpentry of it), and Mary Oliver (the single best reader of her work aloud I have ever seen, in many years of listening to writers try to connect to audiences), and Australia's Helen Garner (who is utterly fascinated in her work by "the ragged hole between ethics and the law," as she says), and Annie Dillard (a genius with a startlingly deep gravelly amused voice), and Ursula Le Guin (who is tiny and brilliant and we ought to admit right here that she is one of the finest writers in American history), and the late Andre Dubus the Second (the best Catholic writer since Flannery O'Connor and J.F. Powers, I believe), and Allan Gurganus (who is gentle and hilarious in person), and Jan Morris (who writes the most graceful lucid limpid prose of anyone alive, I think), but this morning I would like to celebrate one smiling brilliance among many: Cynthia Shoshana Ozick, of the Borough of the Bronx, where she was born on April 17, some years ago.

I once shared a stage with her, during which my role was to choose and ask questions from the audience, a task I immediately flubbed, for I could not resist asking this deeply devout Jewish mystic an ancient Catholic Boy Question, 'If God is all-powerful, can he make a rock so big not even He can lift it?,' to which she gave the right answer, which is giggling.

But before and after that moment (yet another selfish moment for me, amusing only myself), I was transfixed by her wit and erudition, her lack of arrogance, her silver intelligence, her soaring insistence on story as the crucial act of reverence, civilization, community — all the things that fill her work to overflowing. So this morning I send us all back to the work of one of the finest writers ever born in our rich and blessed country; in fact, I assign homework. Read the terrific essayist — choose any one of her alliteratively titled collections *Art and Ardor, Metaphor & Memory, Fame & Folly,* or *Quarrel & Quandary.* (As an editor I would have pushed for her to complete a set of 22 more collections along those lines.) Read the fictioneer: start with her searing brief masterpiece *The Shawl,* and then read *The Messiah of Stockholm* or the wry and haunting *Puttermesser Papers.* Or, for a greatest-hits leap into her work if you have never read a page of it, find the excellent *Cynthia Ozick Reader,* and open it anywhere.

And let us conclude by joining together, in every office and den and subway and breakfast table where you are reading this note, by briefly humming happy birthday to Ms. Ozick, and wishing her health and peace, and thanking her for her gift to us — unforgettable, graceful, sinewy, honest, blunt, lyrical stories. Madame Author, you used your capacious gifts to wonderful effect, for which we thank you, most sincerely.

The Poem Is Everything Else *Except* the Lines on the Page

I have a friend who calls himself a poet because he published a poem in a magazine once, but then for fun he published the exact same poem in another magazine, just to see if he could, and ever since it's been the deluge. By his count he has published the exact same poem in eleven little magazines and journals and reviews and webzines so far. He has published no other poem in his poetic career than that poem, which I have to say is a pretty good poem, although reading it over eleven times, as I have, dilutes the salt and song of it a little — I know where the surprises are, the twists of phrase, the way he cracks his lines so they have a little extra pop and swerve in them. Still, though, as he likes to say, it's a pretty good poem, serviceable, sturdy, not too self-absorbed and self-obsessed and self-indulgent like so many poems are, and as there are no sudden phrases in French or Greek, which happens sometimes in arty poems, and when that linguistic crime occurs, as he says, you want to get a serious baseball bat and have at the ankles of the arty poet for being such a pretentious doofus, although cracking poets on the ankles for being such narcissistic dolts is frowned upon, even by editors, some of whom actually do have baseball bats in their offices, in case of emergencies.

I have asked my friend why he is so intent on publishing this one poem over and over again and he pretty much has a different answer every time I ask the question. Sometimes he says he thinks it is a damned fine poem and the more times it appears the better, on principle. Sometimes he says it's an indictment of our culture that so few people read poems that no one yet has noticed that he publishes the same poem over and over again. Sometimes, on dark days, he says I guess I am not much of a poet, because it looks like all I have is the one poem in me and I am wedded to it until death do us part. Sometimes he says he is playing a shell game with poetry magazine editors, and he does not feel bad about that because it's not like he is getting paid anyways. Sometimes he says his calculus is that poetry magazines are read by so few people that each time the poem is published it is read by a maximum of seven people and therefore the poem has been read by 77 people to date, excluding him and me, and he will quit when he gets over a hundred readers total, including him and me. Sometimes he says that the poem is actually different each time it appears because it is printed in a different typeface or on a different weight of paper or different electric screen, and context is everything in poetry, and therefore the poem is by definition a new poem, given its new context. Sometimes he says that the poem is actually different every time because we are wrong to think that we know anything certain about something we have read before; for one thing we immediately forget most of what we read, and for another the *whole* point of a poem is to have layers and hints and intimations and subtexts and shimmers and suggestions of other meanings and depths, so each time you read the same poem it is not the same poem because you are reading it a different way, on a different day, and of course you are not the same person you were when you read it before either, so how could the poem be the same if you are different when you read it?

Which is a pretty good point, actually.

My friend also says look, the whole point of a poem is to jazz your perceptions, to send you sideways mentally and emotionally for a moment, to stimulate you to see things in a slightly different and ideally refreshing way, so really he is doing readers and editors a subtle service in presenting a poem that you can read in lots of different ways depending on what sort of paper or screen it is appearing on, and the typeface, and the time of day, and who you are when you read it. If you think about this carefully for a moment, he says, I am turning the whole dynamic around, so that the poem is the same but everything else is different; in a sense the poem is no longer the lines on the page or screen, but the whole panoply of things that are different each time the poem appears in a new magazine or journal or review or webzine. The poem is everything else except the lines on the page, get it?

This is a pretty interesting point, actually, but every time he explains this slowly and carefully to me with that glint in his eye I am not sure if he is making a brilliant and subtle point about poetry and art and perception and metaphysical existence or if he has gone over the edge altogether and I am being sold a pile of nuts. So, in classic editorial fashion, I will leave this question to you, the reader, and tiptoe gently out of the end of this essay, leaving you to ponder this metaphysical conundrum on your own while I get a lovely dry ale.

Seantences

It is only after a book of mine is published that I can sit quietly and think *What was* that *all about*?, for during the headlong writing of it I am thinking only about what happens next, and then what I have to cut, and then about all the tiny mistakes (I have the odd habit of mixing up the names of my characters, which makes my editor moan helplessly), and then about what parts might be good to read aloud, and then about how to explain the mistakes, which I cheerfully blame on the Tea Party. But then there comes a time when I can ponder, for a while, the unconscious urge that drove the book — the dreams, the inchoate inspiration, the subconscious energy. And this morning, staring at a novel I wrote about the sea, I realize that this novel began when I was a boy growing up near the ocean, fascinated and frightened by it, absorbed and thrilled, mesmerized and scared. I can remember puttering in the surf with my brothers at age four or so, and even then being riveted by the *endless* of it, the way that it had no confinement, the way that even its horizon was an illusion, the way that it was reputed to be filled with astounding creatures beyond our counting and our ken.

The allure of the sea only grew as I became a reader, and fell headlong into Kipling's *Captains Courageous*, and Jack London's *The Sea Wolf* and *The Cruise of the Snark*, and Robert Louis Stevenson's *Kidnapped* and *In the South Seas*, and Thor Heyerdahl's *Kon-Tiki*, and Joshua Slocum's *Sailing Alone Around the World*, and Melville's *Typee* and *Omoo*, and C.S. Forester's Hornblower novels, Conrad's *Typhoon* and *Youth*, and Robert Gibbings' *Over the Reefs and Far Away*, and the terrific *Mutiny on the Bounty* trilogy by James Norman Hall and

Charles Nordhoff, and every other book I could find in the Merrick Library with blue covers that smacked of sun and salt and spray and storms and sailing and battles at sea and sea-life and voyages on the Mother of All Things.

Though I never went to sea, and do not fish, and am still scared to be more than waist-deep in the ocean, my utter absorption with the sea never did end, and I have happily read hundreds of maritime books over the years, most recently the excellent Richard Bolitho novels of Alexander Kent and the vast 20-volume masterpiece that is the story of Jack Aubrey and Stephen Maturin, by the late Patrick O'Brian; and on the pile of books to read by the bed at home I find not one but two books by James Norman Hall about the South Seas (*Under a Thatched Roof* and *Lost Island*); and so I sit here this morning smiling, for now I see that the novel I thought took two years for me to write took more than fifty, and may well be said to have begun on a bright beach long ago, as a boy of four gazed out at the biggest entity on earth, a vast story that never ends.

Catholic Journalism: a Note

Before the age of Catholic magazines as I have known them for forty years vanishes altogether into a blizzard of bells and digits, and Catholic periodicals assume their future form as shining holograms arising not unlike angels from your computer screen, let us remember and celebrate some of the sweet wild insane moments of the past, so that our children's children will know that once there were small giants like Robert Burns of *U.S. Catholic* magazine, whose suit was always gray and whose face always a shining rosy color especially when he lost his temper, and Peggy Steinfels of *Commonweal* magazine, who looked cherubic and warm but who was eight times more acerbic than any nine bishops, and the Reverend George Hunt of *America* magazine, whose opening essay was so lyrical and funny and eloquent that I knew a man who subscribed to *America* only for George's essay, which he cut from the magazine with a steak knife, sliding the rest of the issue into his parakeet's cage, where he said Jesuit philosophy would for once for God's sake be useful.

And there was Father Louis Miller of *Liguori* magazine, a brief cheerful energetic soul whose secret dream, I think, was that his beloved Redemptorist order would convert all of Latin America and then move slowly and surely north to reclaim the Lutheran enclaves of the upper Midwest; and there was Father John Reedy of *Ave Maria* magazine, who sailed across the campus of Notre Dame accompanied by a black dog the size of a municipality, on which, no kidding, you could have easily placed five small children with room to spare; and there were the harried editors of Franciscan and Maryknoll and Dominican and Paulist and Marianist periodicals, whom I met occasionally at conferences; I could never remember their names, as they seemed silent and bedraggled, and had been sent to the conferences, which were always held in rooms painted orange, to recruit advertising which they knew would never come their way; and so they went home after the conferences on long silent buses, clutching their melancholy satchels; I made a point of watching them board the buses, the poor creatures, always in a gentle rain, or a graying snow, if we were north of Kentucky.

Then there were the editors of diocesan newspapers, another harried and slender bunch; they were always hungry, and would attack the breakfast buffet with grim intent, storing away muffins in their satchels, and drinking so much orange juice their skin grew brighter as the conferences went on; it seemed to me they were not paid by their bishops in money so much as in promises or prayers, and the magazine editors generally would quietly take up a collection for them, or sometimes arrange for a second spread of muffins — an act of kindness I never forgot, and have often remembered as a specific example of the gospels in action in our lives today.

Finally there were the editors of newsletters, and these were men and women so nearly transparent as to be veritable wraiths and hallucinations; if by rare chance there was a brief burst of sunlight at a conference center, the newsletter editors would very nearly vanish, and only the glint of their free pens and coffee cups would give away their presence in the meeting room. Nothing could be done for the newsletter editors, who well knew that not a single soul ever read any of their issues, not one; but it was cheering to visit their sample tables, and paw through their shining eight-page productions, and see them weep silently in joy at having been briefly apprehended. As my career as a Catholic journalist went on I made more and more of an effort to visit the newsletter editors' sample tables, initially just to hear their gentle twittering, not unlike the fowls of the air, but later in something like empathy; an editor's worst fear — indeed such a dark fear that we do not often voice it aloud — is that no one will read or even skim that which you have so assiduously labored upon, argued with the publisher about, and poured your heart into. There is so much work unwitnessed in the world at large, that to fail to witness just the small sea of Catholic journalism in my time would have been a sin, however small; but I tried to see it, and now you have too. Bless you for that.

Review: *Bin Laden's Bald Spot & Other Stories,* by Brian Doyle

I have been reviewing books for newspapers and magazines for twenty years now, and in the course of those years I have written gibbering elegies for extraordinary books, polite insults for selfish books, courteous evasions for poor books by terrific writers, selective paeans for books in which there are nuggets of glory amid a sea of muddle, and other such endless angles on what is, it seems to me, really an interesting sub-genre itself of Literature, a sub-genre with its own masters, the late Christopher Hitchens, for example, not to mention the late John Updike, who was a far better writer *about* novels than he was a writer of them.

But in my entire reviewing career, such as it is, I have never read such a peculiar and maddening book as *Bin Laden's Bald Spot and Other Stories,* which (a) only has about two entire paragraphs in its 140 pages devoted to His Late Murderousness' epic bald spot; (b) has a cover featuring a woman in red shoes with an American flag umbrella, though red shoes and a flag umbrella never appear anywhere in the book; (c) contains some sentences that go on for weeks at a time; (d) insults the late great Gregory Peck on page 2, without subsequent apology *anywhere*; (e) contains a story about the late Joseph Kennedy which never once mentions Mr Kennedy's name, leaving the reader floundering as to whether the story is about Howdy Doody or James Boswell or *what*; (f) contains a story that avidly and repeatedly insults

His Eminence Bernard Cardinal Law, former archbishop of Boston, calling His Eminence the Patron Saint of Rapists, and a criminal, and a slime, and a coward, and a fool who ought to be sentenced to cleaning bathrooms twelve hours a day, and other terrible things like that; (g) contains three hilarious basketball stories that sure seem to be totally true, and how can you call true stories fiction, is that allowed?; (h) contains a story about a ten-kilometer road race in which all the runners are cuckolds, as if *that* could ever happen; (i) contains a story about a man changing his automobile insurance from American Automobile Association regular coverage to American Automobile Association plus coverage, which seems awfully like a plug for the American Automobile Association; (j) contains a story in which Leonard Bernstein is said to have been the size of a poodle, which sounds vaguely insulting, not that there's anything wrong with poodles; (k) contains a story in which apparently the ampersand is the hero of the story, which is confusing; (l) contains a story in which a man boards a bus on which the only other passengers are former boyfriends of his wife, as if *that* could ever happen; (m) contains several stories that are only two or three pages long, so that just as you get into the swing of things they end, which hardly seems fair; (n) contains a story that looks suspiciously like a one-act play; and (o) some other problems which I cannot remember because I am fixated on the fact that in the course of 140 pages this author manages to insult Gregory Peck, Leonard Bernstein, and Bernard Cardinal Law. Has he not heard that there are *women* on this planet also? Are there no women suitable for insulting in even such a slim volume as this? Could he not have devoted even a *line* to the preening of Sarah Palin or the egotism of Ayn Rand? And where is any sort of attention to *diverse* insult? In the space of 25 stories was there no room at all for insulting the arrogance of the Reverend Al Sharpton, the maniacal narcissism of the late Hugo Chavez, or the prim lowercaseness of bell hooks? How hard would it have been to tease bell hooks by simply typing Bell Hooks? But no.

I have read each of Mr Doyle's other books carefully, and I can say without fear of contradiction that there are some passages among them that are not altogether bad; he is a decent essayist; his nonfiction books about wine and hearts are, at least, diverting, and *excellent* bathroom reads; and his novels, while headlong, can certainly be said to be among the best million novels ever published in our estimable country. But of this new fictional direction of his I can say only this without fear of contradiction: it's better than a stick in the eye.

On Failing to Properly Return a Terrific Book by Jan Morris

Went to return a book to the library the other day and it refused to go in the BOOKS ONLY slot. Odd. I tried again several times, thinking perhaps I had suddenly aged beyond belief and could not muster the muscle to cram it through the wall, but no, it was the book itself, adamant, recalcitrant, bristling and ruffling indignantly, that would not allow itself to be returned.

This was a conundrum unlike any I had known before, and o dear lord have I known conundra. I could tell you stories all day and night and most of Tuesday.

I tried the return bin in the library parking lot, a steel tank big as a refrigerator where I have seen many unusual things, among them a small boy climbing into the bin to see what it was like inside, people tossing books at the maw of the bin from moving cars, and a man with a ball-peen hammer attacking the bin for reasons that remain murky.

But again the book refused to be returned.

I should perhaps note that this was the first volume of Jan Morris's magisterial *Pax Brittanica* trilogy, *Heaven's Command*, an unbelievably great book, the single best-written history I have ever read, and this includes William Manchester's glorious first two volumes about Winston Leonard Spencer-Churchill, which remain superb even though I cannot forgive Manchester for dying on me before he finished the third and concluding volume. The nerve of the man.

I tried the AUDIOVISUAL ONLY slot in the adjoining gaping

steel bin in the parking lot, to no avail, and then tried the AUDIOVI-
SUAL MATERIAL ONLY AND WE *MEAN* IT slot by the front door,
looking around carefully to see if there were any slimy little kids who
would rat on the strange man stuffing books into the wrong slot,
but there weren't any, not even the usual ubiquitous Girl Scouts with
their rickety card tables and boxes of howling sugar and those evil laser glares they deliver when you say airily that you bought fifty boxes
yesterday, they can smell lies, you know, like wolves do, and did you
know there are *ten million* Girl Scouts worldwide, try to think of *that*
without a shiver of fear as you crawl into bed tonight.

I thought about just heaving the book at the door of the library
and shuffling away briskly, pretending to scour the heavens for fal-
cons and rockets, but that would be a disservice to the holy librarians,
and it was a moist day also, and no man in his right mind would leave
a genius like Jan Morris out in the rain, so I tried to stuff the slot one
last time, this time with as much of a manful effort as I could muster,
which wasn't much, which made me think ruefully of the Girl Scouts
again, so I sat down to ponder.

There was a powerful temptation to blame Jan Morris for this turn
of affairs, but she's Welsh, and you can't insult such a heroic muddy
nation, and she's the finest writer in the world, not to mention by
all accounts the absolute soul of gentle courtesy, and then I thought
about blaming the Girl Scouts somehow, but then it occurred to me
to wonder why the book was so adamant about not being returned.

Because I am afraid no one will ever check me out again, said
the book suddenly. I was wondering when you would ask. Because I
am not stupid and all this talk about the whole world going utterly
digital gives me the roaring willies. I don't want to be kindled. I don't
want to be electrified. I like the heft and thud and thump of me, the
smell and substance. I like traveling in cars and planes. I like beds
and couches and beaches. I like hands and bellies. I like kids poking
into me by accident. I like the cheerful mind who made me. I like that
she scribbled me in inks of various colors in notebooks of various

shapes in more countries than she can remember. I like that they printed thousands of me with paper and type and glue and thread and cloth. I like the crumbs and coffee people spill on me. I like the way people flitter their fingers along my shelf-mates and alight on me and pull me down and flip me open and get absorbed and have to hustle to borrow me when the librarians bark the time. I liked being borrowed and not downloaded. I like being in the trunk of your car and being read in pubs and hotels and dens. I like kids' voices in the other room from where I am being read. I like being stacked by the bed with Pico Iyer and Silver Surfer comics and the Bible. I have lived in this library for forty years and I'll be damned if I will go back in there to molder until the revolution converts me and my friends into digital bits. I know what I am about, and if the British Empire stood for anything it stood for making dreams real by force of will and character, and I dream of being held by hands and heads and hearts until my pages melt in the rain and the words in me dissolve into dust. Any questions?

I sat there dumbfounded, as you can well imagine, and then I went home and did the only sensible thing to do, which was to write to Jan Morris. She replied immediately, the soul of gentle courtesy. "Try returning it at the same time as you donate my newest book," she wrote, which I did, and this worked, which is something to think about, and so we come to the end of this essay, carefully looking both ways for Girl Scouts.

The New Book

I have been traveling lately, and came back to my office this morning, and opened the mail tottering on my desk, and at the bottom, sturdily holding up the bills and complaints and insults, was a thick packet from a publisher. I open this and take out a gleaming new book. It is redolent and the slipcover is crisp and unwrinkled and the cover rings like true wood when I knuckle it. The weight of the paper inside is just right, so that the pages are substantive but not glossy, and they hold the engravings and maps well, and the pages turn easily, without me having to moisten a finger. The inside front cover précis of the book is refreshingly honest, telling me the bones of the story without overmuch ado. The bio note on the writer is admirably brief and does not feature a photograph of the author posing with his cat or in wrestling togs or in front of a cord of wood which he apparently cut with his bare hands. The blurbs are entertaining and do not claim that this book is way better than the Bible, which is narratively incoherent in the first half and a gnomic quest novel in the second part. There are no typographical errors that I can see on first glance. The cover makes sense, given the contents, and the designer did not try to be cool or hip or dashing, or splurge on pink and yellow. There is blessedly no subtitle. Perhaps best of all, the book ends at around 300 pages, which means that you could actually read it, rather than leave it on the shelf for 50 years and then leave it to your children for them to not read, as we do with Proust.

How very tempting to sit down and begin to read it on the spot; but I wrote it, and remember it very well; I lived in it for two years, and wheedled and coddled and argued with the characters, and delighted and winced at their actions, and even now, a year after turning them over to the publisher, feel a sort of rough love for them. But now they have sailed away from my harbor, and into these lovely pages, between these deftly made covers, and all I can do is be proud of them as they go, and wish them well, and hope they will make many friends on their own. And then I prepare for another subtle literary joy: I slip the book in my bag to carry home, to show my lovely bride and our children the very first copy of my new book.

Unpublished Snippets from an Interview with the Author His Holiness Pope Benedict XVI

Have you now, or have you in the past, tipped over a cow?
I...don't recall.

What is your prime concern when dressing for the funeral of a leader in another religious tradition, i.e. Jewish?
White socks or red. But then you really want to start thinking about car keys, pocket cash for the bar at the reception, and business cards.

Have you ever just totally cruised through a day, pretending to look busy but really spending your time, say, wondering how the White Sox could possibly just steal a title like that?
Well...you have off days, like anyone else. You have days when you just are not bringing your A game. I find, personally, that I perform best when I am feeling a little under the weather. I think it has to do with lowered expectations. I'm not revealing any secrets when I say that there's a lot of pressure in the job. Celebrating Mass for a million people in a field is no walk in the park. Footwork is crucial, and the considered pause. And maybe most important of all is enunciation. Also wear bright colors. How in God's name did the White Sox actually do that? You think about that too? I think about that every day.

People who say they do not perceive miracles loose in this vale of tears are not following the White Sox.

Hobbies, forms of relaxation?
Kick-boxing. A couple or five ales here and there, but only in summer usually. I also have a thorough collection of Silver Surfer comics. I like Puccini records. Slasher movies. The Who, of course.

If you were a vegetable, what vegetable would you be?
Oh, eggplant. That's an easy one.

Best friend?
My boy John Paul II was a dear friend — we used to kid about getting tattoos, but we never got around to it. He had a nasty sense of humor for a playwright. You know playwrights, all self-important and mysterious and all, but he didn't have hardly any of the brooding artist thing going. Plus he was very hip to the fact that playwrights are like poets, no one actually reads their stuff and they don't get paid. John Paul — Jack, I should say — used to say he went into the pope business just to get by. I miss the dude.

What's on your reading table, Your Holiness?
Not Dan Brown, heh heh. But, seriously, there are some things you might expect — I like the thorny language of the King James Bible, even without Wisdom, as it were, and I try to stay up on world politics and religious currents. The most fun for me, reading-wise, are the personal projects I set myself — the complete works of Tiki Barber, for example. Also sometimes when I am feeling cocky and too sure of myself I inflict penance in the form of forced readings — the poetry of James Joyce, anything by Jerzy Kozinski, Saint Augustine. I mean, really, everyone bows and salaams when you say Augustine, but who really reads the guy? He's impenetrable. I think maybe only his mom ever read everything he wrote. That's how she got to be a saint, heh heh.

Ever robbed a liquor store?
Not recently, heh heh.

Do you do your own laundry, Holy Father?
No no — that's why they invented the Curia.

What's the deal with you and small-bore firearms?
Target pistols are why God invented cats.

Favorite saint?
Oh, Catherine of Siena, that's easy. You remember she said when she spoke with God He didn't like to be interrupted and she could hardly get a word in. Who knew the Creator was a monologue guy? That cracks me up.

The whole division-among-Christian-sects thing, you want to speculate a little about that?
Lovely weather these past weeks — hot during the day but crisp enough after sunset for a jacket, you know? Starting to be football weather.

Ever play football, Your Holiness?
Played linebacker for two years in school but then the other guys kept growing and I stopped right about here, which is decent size for a pope but not for a guy anchoring a defense. You need a guy in the middle with some serious attitude and a chest like a refrigerator.

Were you dating anyone at that time?
Not seriously, no.

Your meeting with Hans Kung was widely reported in the Catholic press — would you care to share some of the conversation?
Well, Hans played some football also, mostly tight end — he had the

height, you know, and those big hands. We talked some ball, had a couple of beers. Hans is alright — for a theologian, heh heh.

Last thoughts you want to share with the readers?
Be not afraid. My boy Jack nailed that one good.

Józef Korzeniowski: a Note

Some years ago my lovely bride and I had the incredible luck to house-sit a vast old house by the sea. This was one cool house for any number of reasons; it was rent-free for us for ten months, as the owner and her family only came back in summer; it had a coterie of maintenance men assigned to it and paid ahead of time by the owner, so my job was to sit on the porch and smoke cigars; it was ringed by a small wood in which there were pheasants and night-herons; it was flanked on one side by a genius artist and on the other by a lovely old church; and it had the greatest personal library I had ever seen, *thousands* of books, among which I discovered complete sets of three writers: Winston Churchill, Charles Dickens, and Joseph Conrad.

This posed an immediate problem. None of the three were parsimonious with their works; all of them had their glowing virtues, and one had been a partner in saving civilization from slavery; but even I, then in the full flush of youthful arrogance, knew that I could not read all of all of them in ten months, or even all of two of them. I would have to choose one, I told my lovely bride; but which one?

Sensibly she asked why I had to choose one to read in toto when I could read some of all, or even graze freely among all the books in the house, but I was and am a man, and therefore willing and able to set off on vast silly projects, so I did.

First I decided to test each man by reading the first chapters of three of their books. Churchill showed early promise, but then I dipped into *A History of the English-Speaking Peoples*, possibly the most boring book in the history of the English-speaking peoples, and stopped cold. Dickens had me through *Great Expectations* and *A Tale of*

Two Cities, but then I ran into *Bleak House*, and froze. With trepidation I turned to Conrad, fearing that my lovely bride was right and all I could do those ten months was read the greatest hits of the house... but no! *Youth, Typhoon, Lord Jim, The Shadow Line, The Nigger of the Narcissus*, all superb! and then, deliberately, with my heart in my mouth, I read *The Secret Agent* and *Nostromo*, hoping that he would be as good on land as he was at sea, and he was! And then, blessedly, delightedly, every night in my little study lined with the works of the historian Page Smith, who had lived and worked in the house, I read most of the astonishing outpouring of stories and novels and novellas and essays Joseph Conrad published between 1895 and his death in 1924, including his lovely collection of personal essays *The Mirror of the Sea*.

We had to leave that house at the end of June, as the gracious owner and her clan returned for high summer by the sea, and there is much I miss about it even now — the croak of pheasants in thickets, the plethora of bedrooms (fifteen!) for awed houseguests, the cheerful burly pastor next door, the friendly repairmen with whom I shared cigars, the lovely loneliness of life in a free mansion with my paramour when we were young; but also I miss the patent joy of spending almost a year with one extraordinary writer, who never once disappointed me, even over the course of some thirty books. Offhand I can think of only Graham Greene and Georges Simenon and maybe John Steinbeck for that sort of quality over a long shelf of books; how rare it is to be very good *and* very productive; and how rarely today do we stop and salute and celebrate Józef Teodor Konrad Korzeniowski, born in what is today the seething Ukraine, who unquestionably is one of the finest writers in the history of the English-speaking peoples — all due respect to Sir Winston.

"...These the Visions of Eternity..."

There are, and have been, many fine poets of nature, and William Blake (1757-1827) wasn't one of them. This wonderful English poet, painter, and printer spent 69 of his 72 years in gritty and grimy London, where he was more apt to write of chimney-sweeps than chimney swifts, although he did walk regularly in Hampstead Heath, often remarking its verdure; and the London of Blake's day was much smaller in scope, so a long walk from his house (he lived, variously, on Green Street, Broad Street, Poland Street, South Molton Street, and in the Strand) would take him quickly into the countryside. Still, Blake was hardly a poet of field and forest — except in the three years that he and his wife Catherine left London.

In 1800 matters conspired to bring the Blakes to Felpham, near Chichester on the south coast. The journey was arduous (they left at dawn, changed chaises six times, carried with them 16 heavy boxes and portfolios, and arrived just before midnight), yet "all was Chearfulness & Good Humour on the Road," and that night they tucked in at their thatched cottage with joy.

The cottage was two minutes from the ocean, and Blake was immediately overwhelmed by a riot of animate and vegetative life on a scale he had never seen: clematis, elms, thyme, larks. He was also entranced by the sea, another creature he had never seen; in its "shifting lights" he saw spirits and the luminous "majestic shadows" of great poets and prophets. All in all, "the sweet air & the voices of winds, trees & birds, & the odours of the happy ground, makes [Felpham] a dwelling for immortals," he wrote a friend. "Felpham is a sweet place for Study, because it is more Spiritual than London. Heaven opens here on all sides her golden Gates; her windows are not obstructed by vapours; voices of Celestial inhabitants are more distinctly heard, & their forms more distinctly seen; & my Cottage is also a Shadow of their houses."

Although furiously busy with the printing and engraving projects by which he made his living (one of which was a set of 12 engravings for a friend's poem called *Ballads founded on Anecdotes Relating to Animals*), he set to work on an epic poem called *Milton*. In this work, named for the great blind English poet who wrote *Paradise Lost*, we find, unexpectedly, a nature poet of remarkable perception. *Milton* is a curious and difficult poem, often impenetrable, and all that most readers know of it is the famous stanza with which it opens ("And did those feet in ancient time / Walk upon England's mountains green ..."), a small stand-alone poem which, later set to music as a hymn, serves today as an English national anthem. But *Milton* is the book in which a great burst of nature poetry erupted from this most urban of poets, and the selections on these pages are drawn primarily from that extraordinary work.

For William, most his time in the country was utter joy. He was refreshed as an artist, as he wrote to his dear friend Thomas Butts: "One thing of real consequence I have accomplish'd by coming into the country, which is to me consolation enough: namely, I have recollected all my scatter'd thoughts on Art & resumed my primitive & original ways of Execution in both painting & engraving, which in the confusion of London I had very much lost & obliterated from my mind."

He regained his ordinarily sharp ear for poetic dictation from the heavens: "I have composed an immense number of verses on One Grand Theme, Similar to Homer's *Iliad* or Milton's *Paradise Lost*, the Persons & Machinery intirely new to the Inhabitants of Earth... I have written this Poem from immediate Dictation, twelve or sometimes twenty or thirty lines at a time, without Premeditation & even against my Will; the Time it has taken in writing was thus render'd Non Existent, & an immense Poem Exists which seems to be the Labour of a long Life, all produc'd without Labour or Study. I mention this to show you what I think the Grand Reason of my being brought down here."

He even was an interested observer of a fairy funeral, as he explained years later to a startled woman who happened to sit by him at a social function. "I was walking alone in my garden, there was great stillness among the branches and flowers and more than common sweetness in the air; I heard a low and pleasant sound, and I knew not whence it came. At last I saw the broad leaf of a flower move, and underneath I saw a procession of creatures of the size and colour of green and gray grasshoppers, bearing a body laid out on a rose leaf, which they buried with songs, and then disappeared. It was a fairy funeral."

But the Blakes' stint in the country, which had begun with such promise and Chearfulness, ended poorly. Catherine was ill most of the time, Blake himself was tried for sedition (he tossed an insolent soldier out of his garden, and the embarrassed soldier accused him of threatening to kill King George; Blake was found innocent, but the trial terrified him), and the Felpham friend who had arranged for their country visit (the minor poet William Hayley) turned out to be a well-intentioned but bothersome meddler. So the Blakes hied themselves back to London, where they lived out their days; but from their years in the Sussex country we have some of the most beautiful nature poetry in the English language. "Amen, Hallelujah!" as Blake says in *Milton*.

On Not Saying Yes to the Irrepressible Terence O'Donnell One Night Years Ago When He Said *Hey Let's Get a Beer*

Which probably I should have done, even though at the time my kids were little and my weary wife had been chasing and wrangling and hosing them down all day long and I was already in overtime, as it were, having done a literary event with Terry at the Multnomah County Central Library, during which event he sailed off on a long hilarious story about how he used to run naked through the woods near his cabin in Long Beach, Washington, for medicinal purposes, as he said, because he was convinced that salt air and epic ferns were restorative when applied directly to the skin at high speed; this was before he got crippled and couldn't run anymore, although he claimed to *like* being crippled, all things considered, because it gave him an excuse for a knobby cane, which he loved to brandish, and as he said himself what American Irish writer with any sense of decency would miss the chance to brandish a knobby stick at dogs and cabbies?, which he did, with glee.

After the event at the Multnomah County Central Library, Terence and I were laughing on the steps, and I said this has been a kick, but I better get home, what with all wrangling and hosing duties, and he asked if he could hitch a ride to his apartment on the South Park Blocks, and I said sure, because how often do you get a chance to give a ride to a genius raconteur who has lived in rural Iran for fifteen years and wrote a masterpiece about that, not to mention various other excellent books about Oregon? So we drove the few blocks, Terence telling me tales one after another, and then we sat in the car outside his apartment building for a while, Terence telling me tales one after another, and after about forty riveting stories, Terence said hey let's get a beer, we are deep into the sea of stories now, and I hesitated, and he said I'll even buy the beer, and that almost tipped the moment, free beer being such savory bait, but then I had a vision of my weary wife hosing off the twins on the lawn with the garden hose, and I said nah, I better get home, thanks anyways.

Terence, being a gentleman, said he understood, and he bundled himself out of the car, brandishing his stick, and hobbled into his apartment building, and I drove home, and even now, fifteen years after that night, I think I did the right thing, because your first allegiance, when you are married with small squirming children, is to help out with wrangling and hosing; yet I still wonder what tales Terence might have told over those beers. He was a masterful tale-teller in every way, utterly alert to theatrical gesture and pregnant pause, liable to humor at any moment, vastly traveled, armed with a superb memory, and as well-read a man as I have ever met; and for all his courtliness and gentlemanly ways, he was absorbed by every manner and corner of human life, every shade of social status, every shimmer of emotion and desire. He was one of the greatest storytellers Oregon ever hatched and housed, and he died nine years ago, and I am afraid he is being forgotten, and that is a shame.

His books will always be in libraries here, and his masterpiece *Garden of the Brave in War* will always be in print in America, I suspect; but the salt and song of the man himself, the ocean of his smile, the seethe of his stories, the whip of his wit, the lilt of his laugh, the sheer Portlandishness of the man, the depth of his love for his city and his state — that is dissolving, even as the limping vessel that held his spirit also dissolves into the soil of his beloved Iran, where his ashes are buried. There's a memorial to him in Portland, in the Peace Plaza on his beloved Park Blocks, but the better memorial, especially now as America and Iran brandish sticks at each other, is to read *Garden of the Brave in War*, and to laugh whenever you find a reason to today; consider it a gesture of respect and affection for Terry, a great and wondrous Oregonian.

The Secretary
to the Famous Author
Answers the Morning Mail

Sir: We are in receipt of your invitation to Himself to deliver a talk, but I report sadly that I have been instructed to decline politely, with the usual folderol. I believe he means the usual excuse that he prefers to retain what brief time he has left on this mortal coil for his own work, what little there has been of it in recent years, but he might have meant that he is exhausted creatively, inasmuch as there are no more plots to crib from obscure authors, or that he prefers to spend his time dallying with Miss deWitt instead of sitting his butt in the chair and working at the craft he has so often abused in dismaying and disturbing fashion. I am, sir, and etc.

———

Sir: We are in receipt of your invitation for a cruise on the South Seas during which His duties would be essentially to offer light banter and the occasional authoritative issuance of insufferable and uninformed opinion about the State of Literature Today. I can assure you of his facility to accomplish the latter but I would be reluctant to assure you similarly of the former. I am, sir, and etc.

———

Madame: We are in receipt of your invitation for Himself to deliver an unctuous address to the Friends of Cats at their annual Clawathon event. I am instructed to decline for whatever reasons I can invent without ado, so I will note that cats are the spawn of Satan and the best argument for unregulated handguns. I anticipate your objection, madame, but I must insist from experience that heavier-bore weapons are *not* suitable for suburban use. I am, madame, and etc.

———

Madame: We are in receipt of your invitation for Himself to participate in a panel of learned authors commenting on something having to do with paleontology or pornography, your handwriting not being of the highest order, but I am instructed to decline your most thoughtful offer, unless it is the latter, in which case tell us more. I am, madame, and etc.

———

Sir: We are in receipt of your *awesome* invitation for the surfing event, and, like, decline. Thank you for the sand from the beaches of Mars. I can say without fear of contradiction that we have never received such a gift before.

———

Madame: I assure you that Himself is actually a fervent supporter of the cribbage community in its endless battle against the evil empire of the chess players; no man on earth thinks more highly of your brave and stalwart struggle. But he is by chance absolutely committed to something or other to be determined on the date you mentioned, and could not possibly untangle himself from the wilderness of Miss deWitt.

———

Sir: We are in receipt of your hilarious invitation for Himself to travel, at his expense, across the nation, to seek lodging, at his expense, and sufficiently fortify himself, at his expense, so as to be able to offer a brief public talk, prepared at his expense, for the benefit of your shadowy organization, which, as far as I can tell from the chaos of material you enclosed, would be selling incredibly expensive tickets for the event, the proceeds of which would be beneficial apparently only to you, no evidence of other employees, trustees, or interested parties being discoverable in any of the material you enclosed, not to mention the fact that your organization is not listed anywhere as legal, legitimate, or in fact extant except in the remarkable corridors of your febrile imagination. I am instructed to say yes and make arrangements for Miss deWitt to accompany Him on the journey. I am, sir, and etc.

———•———

Madame: We are in receipt of your courteous invitation for Himself to be a visiting scholar for a year at your estimable institution. I can assure you, madame, that the very concept of Himself making anything but a roaring hash of teaching the young, trying to at least achieve a modicum of civility in committee meetings without foaming at the mouth and trying to grope his neighbors, pretending to responsible management of budget and stipend, remembering to wear pants in public, attempting to rise before noon without infusions of coffee laced with whiskey, refraining from urinating from the campus towers, refraining from using squirrels in trebuchets, muting his usual lewd and lascivious language, or, in fact, answering his own mail, is beyond the reach of imagination as constituted in our species to date. One can only hope for evolution's pace to improve as the years trundle on, their tails dragging slightly in the new-fallen snow.

The Christmas Letter

Greetings and salutations! A quick look at the year past in our family: the Woman of the House started a ska band, had a fistfight with a shopping cart, lost her right eye but then found it again under the couch cushions, and was the object of a terrific crush from one of the two boys who came to the door one day on behalf of the Church of the Risen Lord of the Swamps of the Sewanee. One boy started into a reasoned discussion of spirituality and community as the twin foundational pillars of the Church of the Risen Lord of the Swamps of the Sewanee and the other one just gaped and blubbered until he, this second boy, finally blurted out that she, the Woman of the House, was the very personification of his lifelong dreams of feminine allure, and if she could see her way clear to opening her heart to more than one husband, he, the second boy, could and would adjust his career plan with the Church of the Risen etcetera to include purchasing a ranch in Utah where perhaps societal norms were more open to committed love in other forms than the usual straitjacket of monogamous marriage. The Woman of the House declined but was deeply flattered and made a small contribution to the Church of the Risen etcetera, fine people, as she said later, tall, with excellent teeth. Dental hygiene is *very important*, as she says often, poring over a map of Utah.

Son One did have that unfortunate adventure with a weasel and a pumpkin but we report happily that son and weasel have both recovered, although the pumpkin was lost — a sentence that may never have been written before. Son One also enrolled at laundromat school this fall and has been studying diligently, words that never previously applied to him, but when a young person finds that one powerful driving interest in life, after an adolescence devoted to sneering, underwear catalogues, and expensive software, all you can do is be happy for him, and save your quarters in a pickle jar, isn't that so?

Son Two started out the year on a bodybuilding kick but working only on his left arm for some reason and after he toppled over at the turkey rodeo in McMinnville and had to be hauled home on a boat trailer, he made some life adjustments, and we won't have to build that extra room on the west side of the house, after all! It's such a delight to see your kids come to grips with challenges in life, and bull their way through, whimpering gently and asking for money as if you are made of money, the very idea, do they not have the slightest iota of sense about money? They do not.

Our Lovely Daughter concluded her relationship with Biff, who mournfully then shaved off his mohawk, and we report that we are happy not to have to write or type or say the word Biff anymore, it just isn't a name that a sane mother would inflict on a child, all those consonants at the end comprising, essentially, a lip raspberry, fffffffff, and the name as a whole seeming like something you would name a bison, or a pit bull, or the hero of a penny dreadful novel from the early 1920s. But we are getting distracted here with Biff, and will move along in this letter, but not before once again seizing the chance to excoriate the parents who stared at their new miraculous child, and, probably while drinking heavily, named it Biff. The whole thing makes you revisit the notion that perhaps we should be required to obtain a license to parent, or at least there should be some basic rules for naming a child, like no more than four syllables, and no capital letters in the middle of the name suddenly for no reason, and no naming a child for rainbows or seasons of the year or planets. Also you are not allowed to make up silly words, or name your child something without any vowels, or anything that ends with the letter i, or anything with a space in the middle of it. Nor can you name two or more children with the same name, which is just bad form, and you may not name children for appliances or insects. You may name children for obscure angels and testy minor characters in whatever holy book you keep by the fire, but you must use a capital letter to begin. The rest of the year was lovely and we wish you and yours the best.

Acknowledgments

Many of these essays appeared first in *The Oregonian* newspaper, published in the moist and lovely City of Roses, Stumptown, Puddletown, Bridgetown, old gentle riveting Portland, and I am especially indebted to that excellent newspaper's book editor Jeff Baker for the grace and guts to print such nutty inky adventures. Note Jeff's entertainingly Doylesque introductory essay on page xv. My particular thanks also to Anne Fadiman, Robert Wilson, Sudip Bose, Jean Stipicevic, and Sandra Costich of *The American Scholar*, Ben Schwarz of *The Atlantic*, David Lynn and John Pickard of *The Kenyon Review*, Chip Blake and Hannah Fries of *Orion*, Nancy Boutin of *The Los Angeles Review*, Tim Kroenert of *Eureka Street* (in Melbourne, Australia), John McMurtrie of *The San Francisco Chronicle*, Kim Dana Kupperman of Welcome Table Press (which published "A Note on Playfulnessness" as a lovely little chapbook), Kerry Temple of *Notre Dame Magazine*, and Cathy O'Connell-Cahill of *U.S. Catholic*, which 'posted' (I love that word) "Mister Burns" on its website, as a celebration of that legendary editor of their magazine, which he was, God rest his grinning soul. Editors go to heaven fourth, after mothers, teachers, and nurses.

Brian Doyle

Books by Brian Doyle

FICTION
The Adventures of John Carson
Bin Laden's Bald Spot & Other Stories
Cat's Foot
Chicago
Martin Marten
Mink River
The Plover

NONFICTION
The Grail
The Wet Engine

POETRY AND PRAYER
The Book of Uncommon Prayer
Epiphanies & Elegies
How the Light Gets In
The Kind of Brave You Wanted to Be
A Shimmer of Something
Thirsty for the Joy: Australian & American Voices

BOOKS OF ESSAYS
Children & Other Wild Animals
Credo
Eight Whopping Lies
Grace Notes
Hoops
Leaping
The Mighty Currawongs
Reading in Bed
Saints Passionate & Peculiar
A Sense of Wonder
So Very Much the Best of Us
Spirited Men
Thirsty for the Joy
The Thorny Grace of It
Two Voices (with Jim Doyle)